Exam AZ-800: Adm.... Windows Server Hybrid Core Infrastructure Preparation

Achieve success in your AZ-800 Exam on the first try with our new and exclusive preparation book.

This comprehensive resource is designed to help you test your knowledge, providing a collection of the latest questions with detailed explanations and official references.

Save both time and money by investing in this book, which covers all the topics included in the AZ-800 exam.

This book includes two full-length, highly important practice tests, each with 50 questions, for a total of 100 questions. It also provides detailed explanations for each question and official reference links.

Dedicate your effort to mastering these AZ-800 exam questions, as they offer up-to-date information on the entire exam syllabus.

This book is strategically crafted to not only assess your knowledge and skills but also to boost your confidence for the real exam.

With a focus on thorough preparation, passing the official AZ-800 Exam on your first attempt becomes achievable through diligent study of these valuable resources.

The AZ-800 exam consists of approximately 40 to 60 questions, and candidates are allotted 120 minutes to complete the test.

Skills measured

- Deploy and manage Active Directory Domain Services

(AD DS) in on-premises and cloud environments (30–35%)
- Manage Windows Servers and workloads in a hybrid environment (10–15%)
- Manage virtual machines and containers (15–20%)
- Implement and manage an on-premises and hybrid networking infrastructure (15–20%)
- Manage storage and file services (15–20%)

PRACTICE TEST I

1) Note: This question is part of a series presenting the same scenario. Each question in the series offers a unique solution that might meet the stated objectives. Some sets may have multiple correct solutions, while others may not have any correct solution.

Your network includes an Active Directory Domain Services (AD DS) domain named contoso.com. You need to determine which server is the PDC emulator for the domain.

Solution: In Active Directory Domains and Trusts, you right-click on Active Directory Domains and Trusts in the console tree and select Operations Master.

Does this fulfill the requirement?

A. Yes

B. No

2) Note: This question is part of a series presenting the same scenario. Each question in the series offers a unique solution that might meet the stated objectives. Some sets may have multiple correct solutions, while others may not have any correct solution.

Your network includes an Active Directory Domain Services (AD DS) domain named contoso.com. You need to determine which server is the PDC emulator for the domain.

Solution: At a command prompt, you run netdom.exe query fsmo.

Does this achieve the goal?

A. Yes

B. No

3) You have an on-premises Active Directory Domain Services (AD DS) domain that syncs with an Azure Active Directory (Azure AD) tenant. You plan to implement self-service password reset (SSPR) in Azure AD. To ensure that users who reset their passwords using SSPR can use the new passwords for resources in the AD DS domain, what action should you take?

A. Deploy the Azure AD Password Protection proxy service on the on-premises network.

B. Run the Microsoft Azure Active Directory Connect wizard and enable Password writeback.

C. Assign the Change password permission for the domain to the Azure AD Connect service account.

D. Assign the impersonate a client after authentication user right to the Azure AD Connect service account.

4) You have an Azure Active Directory Domain Services (Azure AD DS) domain named contoso.com. You need to grant an administrator the ability to manage Group Policy Objects (GPOs) while adhering to the principle of least privilege.

Which group should you add the administrator to?

A. AAD DC Administrators

B. Domain Admins

C. Schema Admins

D. Enterprise Admins

E. Group Policy Creator Owners

5) Drag Drop:

You create a new Azure subscription and plan to deploy Azure Active Directory Domain Services (Azure AD DS) along with Azure virtual machines. To ensure that the virtual machines can join Azure AD DS, what three actions should you perform in sequence?

Arrange the actions (a to f) in the correct order (1 to 3):

Actions:

a. Modify the settings of the Azure virtual network.

b. Install the Active Directory Domain Services role.

c. Install Azure AD Connect.

d. Create an Azure virtual network.

e. Create an Azure AD DS instance.

f. Run the Active Directory Domain Service Installation Wizard.

Answer area:

1..

2..

3..

6) HOTSPOT

You have an Azure Active Directory Domain Services (Azure AD DS) domain and you create a new user named Admin1. To allow Admin1 to deploy custom Group Policy settings to all the computers in the domain while adhering to the principle of least privilege, what should you do?

Hot Area:

Answer area:

1. Add Admin1 to the following group:

a. AAD DC Administrators

b. Domain Admins

c. Group Policy Creator Owners

2. Instruct Admin1 to apply the custom Group Policy settings by:

a. Creating a new Group Policy Object (GPO) and linking the GPO to the domain

b. Modifying AADDC Computers GPO

c. Modifying the default domain GPO

7) Drag Drop

Your network has a single-domain Active Directory Domain Services (AD DS) forest named contoso.com, which includes one Active Directory site. You plan to deploy a read-only domain controller (RODC) in a new datacenter using a server named Server1. A user named User1 is a member of the local Administrators group on Server1.

You need to recommend a deployment plan that meets the

following criteria:

- Allows User1 to perform the RODC installation on Server1
- Provides control over the AD DS replication schedule to Server1
- Places Server1 in a new site named RemoteSite1
- Follows the principle of least privilege

Which three actions should you recommend performing in sequence?

To answer, choose the appropriate actions (a to e) from the list of actions to the answer area and arrange them in the correct order (1, 2 and 3).

Select and Place:

Actions:

a. Instruct User1 to run the Active Directory Domain Services installation Wizard on Server1.

b. Create a site and a subnet.

c. Create a site link.

d. Pre-create an RODC account.

e. Add User1 to the Contoso\Administrators group.

Answer area:

1...

2...

3...

8) Your network includes an Active Directory Domain Services (AD DS) domain with 20 domain controllers, 100

member servers, and 100 client computers. You have a Group Policy Object (GPO) named GPO1 that contains Group Policy preferences. You plan to link GPO1 to the domain and need to ensure that the preferences in GPO1 apply only to domain member servers and not to domain controllers or client computers. All other Group Policy settings in GPO1 should apply to all computers.

What type of item-level targeting should you use to achieve this with minimal administrative effort?

A. Domain

B. Operating System

C. Security Group

D. Environment Variable

9) Drag Drop

You have deployed a new Active Directory Domain Services (AD DS) forest named contoso.com. The domain includes three domain controllers: DC1, DC2, and DC3. You have renamed Default-First-Site-Name to Site1 and plan to ship DC1, DC2, and DC3 to different datacenters.

You need to configure replication between DC1, DC2, and DC3 to achieve the following:

- Ensure each domain controller is located in its own Active Directory site.
- Control the replication schedule independently between each site.
- Minimize interruptions to replication.

Which three actions should you perform in sequence in the Active Directory Sites and Services console?

To answer, choose the appropriate actions (a to e) from the list of actions to the answer area and arrange them in the correct order (1, 2 and 3).

Actions:

a. Create a connection object between DC1 and DC2.

b. Create an additional site link that contains Site1 and Site2.

c. Create two additional sites named Site2 and Site3. Move DC2 to Site2 and DC3 to Site3.

d. Create a connection object between DC2 and DC3.

e. Remove Site2 from DEFAULTIPSITELINK.

Answer area:

1...

2...

3...

10) Your network includes an Active Directory Domain Services (AD DS) forest named contoso.com. The root domain has the following domain controllers:

Name	FSMO role
DC1	Domain naming master
DC2	RID master
DC3	PDC emulator
DC4	Schema master
DC5	Infrastructure master

Which domain controller's failure will prevent you from creating application partitions?

A. DC1

B. DC2

C. DC3

D. DC4

E. DC5

11) Your network includes an on-premises Active Directory Domain Services (AD DS) domain named contoso.com. The domain contains the following objects:

Name	Type
User1	User
Group1	Universal security group
Group2	Domain local security group
Computer1	Computer

You plan to synchronize contoso.com with an Azure Active

Directory (Azure AD) tenant using Azure AD Connect. To ensure that all objects can be utilized in Conditional Access policies, what should you do?

A. Select the Configure Hybrid Azure AD join option.

B. Change the scope of Group1 and Group2 to Global.

C. Clear the Configure device writeback option.

D. Change the scope of Group2 to Universal.

12) Your network includes a multi-site Active Directory Domain Services (AD DS) forest, where each site is connected via manually configured site links and automatically generated connections. To reduce the convergence time for changes in Active Directory, what should you do?

A. For each site link, modify the replication schedule.

B. For each site links, modify the site link costs.

C. Create a site link bridge that contains all the site links.

D. For each site link, modify the options attribute.

13) Drag Drop

You deploy a single-domain Active Directory Domain Services (AD DS) forest named contoso.com and add five servers to a group called ITFarmHosts. You plan to set up a Network Load Balancing (NLB) cluster named NLBCluster.contoso.com that will include these five servers.

You need to ensure that the NLB service on the cluster nodes can authenticate using a group managed service account (gMSA).

Which three PowerShell cmdlets should you run in sequence?

To answer, choose the appropriate cmdlets (a to f) from the list of cmdlets to the answer area and arrange them in the correct order (1, 2 and 3).

Select and Place:

Cmdlets:

a. New-ADServiceAccount

b. Install-ADServiceAccount

c. Add-ADComputerServiceAccount

d. Set-KdsConfiguration

e. Add-KdsRootKey

f. Add-ADGroupMember

Answer area:

1..

2..

3..

14) You have an on-premises Active Directory Domain Services (AD DS) domain that syncs with an Azure Active Directory (Azure AD) tenant. Some of your Windows 10 devices are Azure AD hybrid-joined. To enable Windows Hello for Business for users signing into these devices, which optional feature should you enable in Azure AD Connect?

A. Device writeback

B. Group writebeack

C. Azure AD app and attribute filtering

D. Password writeback

E. Directory extension attribute sync

15) HOTSPOT

Your network includes an Active Directory Domain Services (AD DS) forest named contoso.com, which has a child domain named east.contoso.com. You create two users in the contoso.com domain: Admin1 and Admin2.

You need to ensure that:

- Admin1 can create and manage Active Directory sites.
- Admin2 can deploy domain controllers in the east.contoso.com domain.

The solution must adhere to the principle of least privilege.

To which group should you add each user?

To answer, choose the appropriate options in the answer area.

Hot area:

Answer area:

Admin1:

a. Contoso Administrators

b. Contoso\Domain Admins

c. Contoso\Enterprise Admins

d. East Administrators

e. East Domain Admins

Admin2:

a. Contoso Administrators

b. Contoso\Domain Admins

c. Contoso\Enterprise Admins

d. East Administrators

e. East Domain Admins

16) *Note: This question is part of a series with the same scenario. Each question offers a unique solution that may meet the goals. Some scenarios may have more than one correct solution, while others may not have any.*

Your network has an Active Directory Domain Services (AD DS) forest with three sites: Site1, Site2, and Site3, each containing two domain controllers. These sites are interconnected via the DEFAULTIPSITELINK. You have just opened a new branch office with only client computers.

To ensure that client computers in the new branch office are primarily authenticated by the domain controllers in Site1, you configure the following solution: You create an organizational unit (OU) for the client computers in the branch office and apply a Group Policy Object (GPO) with the Try Next Closest Site setting to this OU.

Does this meet the goal?

A. Yes

B. No

17) *Note: This question is part of a series with the same scenario.*

Each question offers a unique solution that may meet the goals. Some scenarios may have more than one correct solution, while others may not have any.

Your network includes an Active Directory Domain Services (AD DS) forest with three sites: Site1, Site2, and Site3, each containing two domain controllers. These sites are connected using DEFAULTIPSITELINK. You have recently opened a new branch office with only client computers.

To ensure that client computers in the new branch office are primarily authenticated by the domain controllers in Site1, you create a new site called Site4 and add Site4 to the DEFAULTIPSITELINK.

Does this meet the goal?

A. Yes

B. No

18) *Note: This question is part of a series with the same scenario. Each question offers a unique solution that may meet the goals. Some scenarios may have more than one correct solution, while others may not have any.*

Your network has an Active Directory Domain Services (AD DS) forest with three sites: Site1, Site2, and Site3, each containing two domain controllers. The sites are interconnected via DEFAULTIPSITELINK. You have recently opened a new branch office with only client computers.

To ensure that the client computers in the new branch office are primarily authenticated by the domain controllers in Site1, you configure the Try Next Closest Site Group Policy Object (GPO) setting in a GPO and link it to Site1.

Does this meet the goal?

A. Yes

B. No

19) *Note: This question is part of a series with the same scenario. Each question offers a unique solution that may meet the goals. Some scenarios may have more than one correct solution, while others may not have any.*

Your network has an Active Directory Domain Services (AD DS) domain named contoso.com. To identify the server that is the PDC emulator for the domain, you open Active Directory Sites and Services, right-click Default-First-Site-Name in the console tree, and select Properties.

Does this meet the goal?

A. Yes

B. No

20) Your network has a single-domain Active Directory Domain Services (AD DS) forest named contoso.com. The forest includes the servers listed in the table below.

Name	Description
DC1	Domain controller
Server1	Member server

You plan to install a line-of-business (LOB) application on Server1, which will include a custom Windows service. A new corporate security policy requires that all custom Windows services operate under a group managed service account (gMSA). After deploying a root key, you need to create, configure, and install the gMSA for the new application.

Which two actions should you perform?

A. On Server1, run the setspn command.

B. On DC1, run the New-ADServiceAccount cmdlet.

C. On Server1, run the Install-ADServiceAccount cmdlet.

D. On Server1, run the Get-ADServiceAccount cmdlet.

E. On DC1, run the Set-ADComputer cmdlet.

F. On DC1, run the Install-ADServiceAccount cmdlet.

21) HOTSPOT:

Your network includes three Active Directory Domain Services (AD DS) forests, as depicted in the following exhibit.

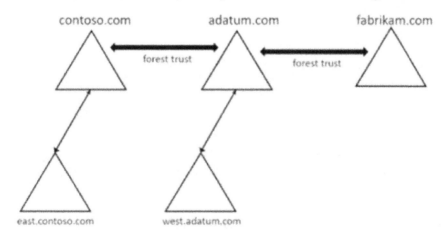

The network contains the users shown in the following table.

Name	Domain
User1	east.contoso.com
User2	fabrikam.com

The network contains the security groups shown in the following table.

Name	Type	Domain
Group1	Domain local	west.adatum.com
Group2	Universal	contoso.com
Group3	Universal	east.contoso.com

For each of the following statements, choose Yes if the statement is true. Otherwise. choose No.

Hot area:

Answer area:

Statements:

1. You can add User1 to Group1.

2. You can add User2 to Group3.

3. You can grant Group2 permissions to the resources in the fabrikam.com domain.

22) Your network includes an Active Directory Domain Services (AD DS) forest named contoso.com. The root domain of this forest has a server named server1.contoso.com. A two-way forest trust is established between the contoso.com forest and another AD DS forest named fabrikam.com, which has 10

child domains.

You need to ensure that only members of the group fabrikam \Group1 are allowed to authenticate to server1.contoso.com.

What should you do first?

A. Add fabrikam\Group1 to the local Users group on server1.contoso.com.

B. Enable SID filtering for the trust.

C. Enable Selective authentication for the trust.

D. Change the trust to a one-way external trust.

23) Your network includes an Active Directory Forest with two domains: contoso.com and east.contoso.com. The forest contains the servers listed in the table below.

Name	Domain	Configuration
DC1	contoso.com	Domain controller
Server1	contoso.com	Member server
DC2	east.contoso.com	Domain controller
Server2	east.contoso.com	Member server

Contoso.com contains a user named User1.
You add User1 to the built-in Backup Operators group in contoso.com.

Which servers can User1 back up?

A. DC1 only

B. Server1 only

C. DC1 and DC2 only

D. DC1 and Server1 only

E. DC1, DC2, Server1, and Server2

24) HOTSPOT:

Your network includes an Azure Active Directory Domain Services (Azure AD DS) domain named contoso.com.

You need to set up a password policy for the local user accounts on the Azure virtual machines that are joined to contoso.com.

What should you do?

To answer, choose the appropriate options in the answer area.

Answer area:

1. Sign in by using a user account that is a member of the:

a. AAD DC Administrators group

b. Administrators group

c. Domain Admins group

2. Use a Group Policy Object (GPO) linked to the:

a. AADDC Computers organizational unit (OU)

b. AADDC Users organizational unit (OU)

c. Computers container

25) SIMULATION:

You need to create a user named Admin1 in contoso.com. Admin1 must be able to back up and restore files on SRV1. The solution must use principle of the least privilege.

To complete this task, sign in the required computer or computers.

26) SIMULATION:

You need to ensure that the minimum password length for members of the BranchAdmins group is 12 characters. The solution must affect only the BranchAdmins group.

To complete this task, sign in the required computer or computers.

27) SIMULATION:

You need to configure a Group Policy preference to ensure that users in the organizational unit (OU) named Server Admins have a shortcut to a folder named \\srv1.contoso.com\data on their desktop when they sign in to the computers in the domain.

To complete this task, sign in the required computer or computers.

28) SIMULATION:

You plan to promote a domain controller named DC3 in a site in Seattle.

You need to ensure that DC3 only replicates with DC1 and DC2 between 8 PM and 6 AM.

To complete this task, sign in the required computer or computers.

29) SIMULATION:

You plan to ensure that DC2 is the schema master for

contoso.com.

To complete this task, sign in the required computer or computers.

30) Your network includes an Active Directory Domain Services (AD DS) forest with three domains, each having 10 domain controllers.

You intend to store a DNS zone in a custom Active Directory partition and want this partition to replicate to only four of the domain controllers.

You need to create the Active Directory partition for the zone and ensure it replicates to the specified domain controllers.

What should you use?

A. Windows Admin Center

B. DNS Manager

C. Active Directory Sites and Services

D. ntdsutil.exe

31) Drag Drop

Your network consists of a single domain Active Directory Domain Services (AD DS) forest named contoso.com, with one Active Directory site.

You plan to deploy a read-only domain controller (RODC) to a new datacenter on a server called Server1. User1, who is a member of the local Administrators group on Server1, will perform the installation.

To ensure compliance with the principle of least privilege and meet the deployment requirements, you need a plan that:

· Allows User1 to install the RODC on Server1
· Places Server1 in a new site called RemoteSite1
· Uses the principle of least privilege

Which three actions should you recommend performing in sequence?

To answer, choose the appropriate actions (a to e) from the list of actions to the answer area and arrange them in the correct order (1, 2 and 3).

Actions:

a. Instruct User1 to run the Active Directory Domain Services installation Wizard on Server1.

b. Create a site and a subnet.

c. Create a site link.

d. Pre-create an RODC account.

e. Add User1 to the Contoso\Administrators group.

Answer area:

1..

2..

3..

32) Your network includes an Active Directory domain named contoso.com. The domain comprises the computers listed in the following table.

Name	Operating system
Computer1	Windows 11
Server1	Windows Server 2016
Server2	Windows Server 2019
Server3	Windows Server 2022

On Server3, you create a Group Policy Object (GPO) named GPO1 and link it to contoso.com. GPO1 contains a shortcut preference called Shortcut1, with item-level targeting configured as shown in the exhibit.

To which computer will Shortcut1 be applied?

A. Server3 only

B. Computer1 and Server3 only

C. Server2 and Server3 only

D. Server1, Server2, and Server3 only

33) Your network consists of a multi-site Active Directory Domain Services (AD DS) forest. Each Active Directory site is connected using manually configured site links and automatically generated connections. You need to reduce the latency for Active Directory changes.

What action should you take?

A. Adjust the site link costs for each site link.

B. Establish a site link bridge that includes all the site links.

C. Alter the options attribute for each site link.

D. Change the replication schedule for each site link.

34) Drag Drop

Your network includes two Active Directory Domain Services (AD DS) forests: contoso.com and fabrikam.com. The contoso.com forest has three child domains— amer.contoso.com, apac.contoso.com, and emea.contoso.com —while the fabrikam.com forest contains a child domain named apac.fabrikam.com. A bidirectional forest trust exists between contoso.com and fabrikam.com.

To grant users in the contoso.com forest access to resources in the fabrikam.com forest, you need to meet the following requirements:

- Users in contoso.com should only be added to groups within the contoso.com forest.
- Permissions for accessing resources in fabrikam.com must be granted only through groups within the fabrikam.com forest.

· Minimize the number of groups used.

Which type of groups should you use to organize the users and to assign permissions?

To answer, choose the appropriate group types (a, b and c) to the correct requirements (1 and 2).

Each group may be used once, more than once, or not at all.

Answer area:

Group types:

a. Domain global

b. Domain local

c. Universal

1. Organize users: ....

2. Assign permissions: ....

35) Hotspot:

Your network includes two Active Directory forests and a domain trust, as depicted in the following diagram.

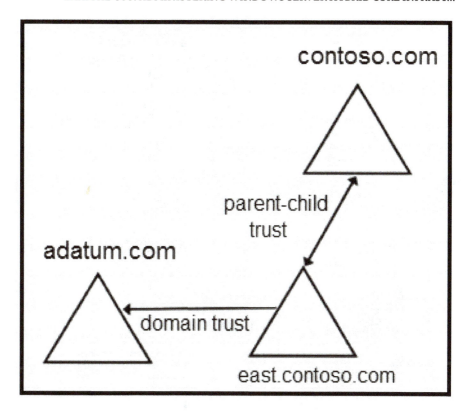

The domain trust has the following configurations:
• Name: adatum.com

• Type: External

• Direction: One-way, outgoing

• Outgoing trust authentication level: Domain-wide authentication

The forests contain the users shown in the following table.

Name	Domain
User1	adatum.com
User2	contoso.com
User3	east.contoso.com

The forests contain the network shares shown in the following table.

Name	In domain
Share1	adatum.com
Share2	contoso.com
Share3	east.contoso.com

For each of the following statements, choose Yes if the statement is true. Otherwise, choose No.

Answer area:

Statements:

1. User1 can be assigned permissions for Share3.

2. User2 can be assigned permissions for Share1.

3. User3 can be assigned permissions for Share1.

36) Hotspot

Your network consists of an Active Directory Domain Services (AD DS) forest named contoso.com, which includes a child domain called east.contoso.com. The network also contains the servers listed in the following table.

Name	Domain	Description
DC1	contoso.com	Has the schema master, infrastructure master, and domain naming master roles
DC2	east.contoso.com	Has the PDC emulator and RID master roles and is a global catalog server
Server1	contoso.com	Has the File Server, DFS Namespaces, and DFS Replication server roles

You need to create a folder for the Central Store to manage Group Policy template files for the entire forest.

What should you name the folder, and on which server should you create the folder?

To answer, choose the appropriate options in the answer area.

Answer area:

1. Name:

a. CentralDefinitions

b. PolicyDefinitions

c. TemplateDefinitions

2. Server:

a. DC1 only

b. DC2 only

c. Server1 only

d. DC1 and DC2 only

e. DC1, DC2, and Server1

37) Hotspot

Your network includes an Active Directory Domain Services (AD DS) domain with the domain controllers listed in the following table.

Name	Description
DC1	Has the schema master, infrastructure master, and domain naming master roles
DC2	Has the PDC emulator and RID master roles and is a global catalog server
DC3	*None*

You need to configure DC3 to be the authoritative time server for the domain.

Which operations master role should you transfer to DC3, and which console should you use?

To answer, choose the appropriate options in the answer area.

Answer area:

1. Role:

a. Domain naming master

b. Infrastructure master

c. PDC emulator

d. RID master

e. Schema master

2. Console:

a. Active Directory Administrative Center

b. Active Directory Domains and Trusts

c. Active Directory Sites and Services

d. Active Directory Users and Computers

38) Drag Drop

Your network includes an Active Directory domain named

contoso.com, which has group managed service accounts (gMSAs). There is a server named Server1, running Windows Server, that operates in a workgroup and hosts Windows containers.

You need to ensure that these Windows containers can authenticate with the contoso.com domain.

Which three actions should you perform in sequence?

To answer, choose the appropriate actions (a to e) from the list of actions to the answer area and arrange them in the correct order (1, 2 and 3).

Actions:

a. On Server1, install and run ccg.exe.

b. On Server1, run New-CredentialSpec.

c. In contoso.com, generate a Key Distribution Service (KDS) root key.

d. In contoso.com, create a gMSA and a standard user account.

e. From a domain-joined computer, create a credential spec file and copy the file to Server1.

Answer area:

1..

2..

3..

39) To sync your on-premises Active Directory domain (contoso.com) with your Azure AD tenant using Azure AD Connect cloud sync, you need to create an account for this purpose.

What type of account should you create for use by Azure AD Connect cloud sync?

A. system-assigned managed identity

B. group managed service account (gMSA)

C. user

D. InetOrgPerson

40) Your network includes an Active Directory Domain Services (AD DS) domain, which contains the domain controllers listed in the following table.

Name	Description
DC1	PDC emulator, RID master, and global catalog server
DC2	Infrastructure master and domain naming master
DC3	Schema master
RODC1	Read-only domain controller (RODC)

You need to ensure that if an attacker compromises the computer account of RODC1, the attacker cannot view the Employee-Number AD DS attribute.
Which partition should you modify?

A. configuration

B. global catalog

C. domain

D. schema

41) Hotspot

Your network includes an on-premises Active Directory Domain Services (AD DS) domain named contoso.com, which

is synchronized with an Azure AD tenant. The tenant has a group called Group1, and the users are listed in the following table.

Name	In organizational unit (OU)
User1	OU1
User2	OU2

Domain/OU filtering in Azure AD Connect is configured as shown in the Filtering exhibit. (Click the Filtering tab.)

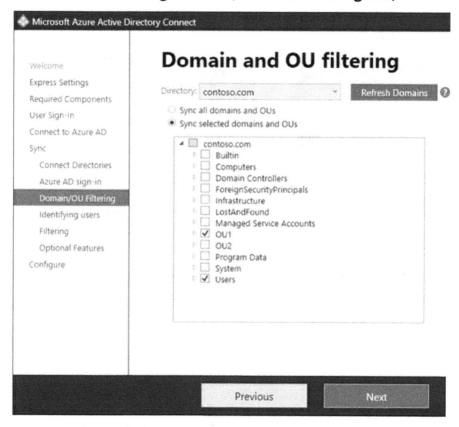

You review the Azure AD Connect configurations as shown in the Configure exhibit. (Click the Configure tab.)

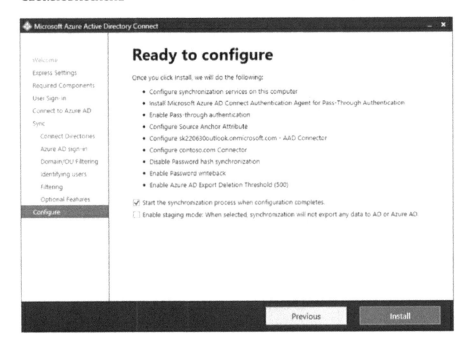

For each of the following statements, choose Yes if the statement is true. Otherwise, choose No.

Answer area:

Statements:

1. User1 can use self-service password reset (SSPR) to reset his password.

2. If User1 connects to Microsoft Exchange Online, an on-premises domain controller provides authentication.

3. You can add User2 to Group1 as a member.

42) Hotspot

Your on-premises network includes an Active Directory Domain Services (AD DS) domain. You plan to synchronize this domain with an Azure AD tenant using Azure AD Connect cloud sync. You need to:

- Install the necessary software for synchronizing the domain with Azure AD.
- Enable password hash synchronization.

What should you install, and what should you use to enable password hash synchronization?

To answer, choose the appropriate options in the answer area.

Answer area:

1. Install:

a. Active Directory Administrative Center

b. Azure AD Connect

c. The AD FS Management console

d. The Azure AD Connect provisioning agent

2. Use:

a. Active Directory Administrative Center

b. Azure AD Connect

c. The AD FS Management console

d. The Azure portal

43) Hotspot

Your network includes two Active Directory Domain Services (AD DS) forests, as depicted in the following diagram.

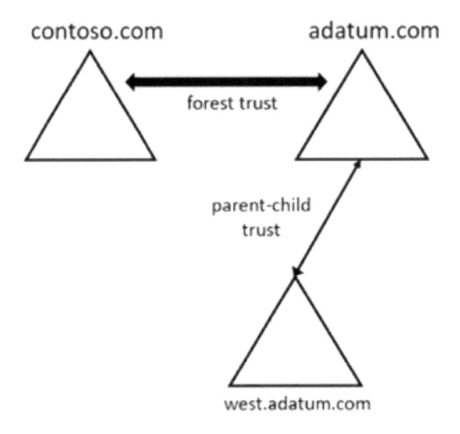

The forests contain the domain controllers shown in the following table.

Name	Domain	Global catalog	Schema master
DC1	adatum.com	Yes	Yes
DC2	adatum.com	No	No
DC3	west.adatum.com	Yes	No
DC4	contoso.com	Yes	Yes

You perform the following actions on DC1:

• Create a user named User1.

• Extend the schema with a new attribute named Attribute1.

To which domain controllers are User1 and Attribute1

replicated?

Answer area:

1. User1:

a. DC2 only

b. DC3 only

c. DC2 and DC3 only

d. DC3 and DC4 only

e. DC2, DC3, and DC4

Attribute1:

a. DC2 only

b. DC4 only

c. DC2 and DC3 only

d. DC2, DC3, and DC4

44) Your network includes an Active Directory Domain Services (AD DS) domain, which contains the resources listed in the following table.

Name	Description
CLIENT1	Client computer that runs Windows
DC1	Domain controller
Server1	File server
Server2	File server

To configure Storage Replica for replicating a volume from Server1 to Server2, where should you install Windows Admin Center?

A. Server1

B. CLIENT1

C. DC1

D. Server2

45) To prevent users from including the word "contoso" in their passwords for an on-premises Active Directory Domain Services (AD DS) domain named contoso.com that syncs with Azure AD using Azure AD Connect, what should you use?

A. Azure Active Directory admin center

B. Active Directory Users and Computers

C. Synchronization Service Manager

D. Windows Admin Center

46) Your network includes an Active Directory Domain Services (AD DS) forest with three domains, each containing 10 domain controllers. You plan to store a DNS zone in a custom Active Directory partition and need this partition to replicate to only four of the domain controllers. How should you create the Active Directory partition for this zone and what should you use?

A. Windows Admin Center

B. Set-DnsServer

C. New-ADObject

D. ntdsutil.exe

47) Hotspot

You have an Active Directory Domain Services (AD DS) domain with a group called Group1. To create a group managed service account (gMSA) named Account1 and ensure that Group1 can use Account1. How should you complete the script?

To answer, choose the appropriate options in the answer area.

(1) "Account" -DNSHostName "website.contoso.com" (2) "Group"

Answer area:

(1)

a. Add-ADComputerServiceAccount

b. Install-ADServiceAccount

c. New-ADObject

d. New-ADServiceAccount

(2)

a-AuthenticationPolicy

b.-Instance

c.-PrincipalsAllowedToDelegateToAccount

d-PrincipalsAllowedToRetrieveManagedPassword

48) You have an on-premises Active Directory Domain Services (AD DS) domain that syncs with Azure AD. After deploying an app that adds custom attributes to the domain, you find that you cannot query these custom attributes from Azure Cloud Shell. To ensure that the custom attributes are

available in Azure AD.

Which task should you perform from Microsoft Azure Active Directory Connect first?

A. Configure device options

B. Manage federation

C. Customize synchronization options

D. Refresh directory schema

49) You have an Active Directory Domain Services (AD DS) domain that includes the domain controllers listed in the table below.

Name	Operations master role
DC1	Schema master
DC2	Infrastructure master
DC3	Domain naming master
DC4	PDC emulator, RID master

The domain contains an app named App1 that uses a custom application partition to store configuration data.

You decommission App1.

When you attempt to remove the custom application partition, the process fails.
Which domain controller is unavailable?

A. DC1

B. DC2

C. DC3

D. DC4

50) Case Study:

Overview:

Company Information:

ADatum Corporation is a manufacturing company with its main office located in Seattle and branch offices in Los Angeles and Montreal.

Fabrikam Partnership:

ADatum has recently formed a partnership with Fabrikam, Inc., another manufacturing company with its main office in Boston and a branch office in Orlando. Both companies plan to collaborate on several joint projects.

Existing Environment:

ADatum AD DS Environment:

ADatum's on-premises network includes an Active Directory Domain Services (AD DS) forest named adatum.com. This forest contains two domains: adatum.com and east.adatum.com, along with the domain controllers listed in the following table.

Name	Domain	Operations master roles
DC1	adatum.com	Schema master
DC2	adatum.com	*None*
DC3	east.adatum.com	PDC emulator, RID master

Fabrikam AD DS Environment

The on-premises network of Fabrikam contains an AD DS

forest named fabrikam.com.

The forest contains two domains named fabrikam.com and south.fabrikam.com.

The fabrikam.com domain contains an organizational unit (OU) named Marketing.

Server Infrastructure

The adatum.com domain contains the servers shown in the following table.

Name	Role
HyperV1	Hyper-V
SSPace1	File and Storage Services

HyperV1 contains the virtual machines shown in the following table.

Name	Operating system	Description
VM1	Windows Server 2022 Datacenter	Joined to the adatum.com domain Contains a file share named Data1 and a local user named User1
VM2	Red Hat Enterprise Linux (RHEL)	Contains a local user named User2
VM3	Windows Server 2022 Standard	Joined to the adatum.com domain Has the File and Storage Services role installed

All the virtual machines on HyperV1 have only the default management tools installed.

SSPace1 contains the Storage Spaces virtual disks shown in the following table.

Name	Number of physical disks	Redundancy
Disk1	8	Three-way mirror
Disk2	12	Parity

Azure Resources

ADatum has an Azure subscription that contains an Azure AD tenant. Azure AD Connect is configured to sync the adatum.com forest with Azure AD.

The subscription contains the virtual networks shown in the following table.

Name	Location	Subnet
VNet1	West US	Subnet1, Subnet2
VNet2	West US	SubnetA, SubnetB

The subscription contains the Azure Private DNS zones shown in the following table.

Name	Virtual network link
Zone1.com	VNet1
Zone2.com	VNet2
Zone3.com	*None*

The subscription contains the virtual machines shown in the following table.

Name	Operating system	Security type
Server1	Windows Server 2022 Datacenter: Azure Edition	Trusted launch
Server2	Windows Server 2022 Datacenter: Azure Edition	Standard
Server3	Windows Server 2022 Datacenter	Standard
Server4	Windows Server 2019 Datacenter	Trusted launch

All the servers are in a workgroup.

The subscription contains a storage account named storage1 that has a file share named share1.

Requirements
Planned Changes

ADatum plans to implement the following changes:

• **Sync Data1 to share1.**

• **Configure an Azure runbook named Task1.**

• **Enable Azure AD users to sign in to Server1.**

• **Create an Azure DNS Private Resolver that has the following configurations:**

• **Name: Private1**

• **Region: West US**

• **Virtual network: VNet1**

• **Inbound endpoint: SubnetB**

• **Enable users in the adatum.com domain to access the resources in the south.fabrikam.com domain.**

Technical Requirements

ADatum identifies the following technical requirements:

• The data on SSPace1 must be available always.
• DC2 must become the schema master if DC1 fails.

• VM3 must be configured to enable per-folder quotas.

• Trusts must allow access to only the required resources.

• The users in the Marketing OU must have access to storage1.

• Azure Automanage must be used on all supported Azure virtual machines.

• A direct SSH session must be used to manage all the supported virtual machines on HyperV1.

DC1 fails.

You need to meet the technical requirements for the schema master.

You run ntdsutil.exe.

Which five commands should you run in sequence?

To answer, choose the appropriate commands (a to f) from the list of commands to the answer area and arrange them in the correct order (1 to 5)?

Commands:

a. seize schema master

b. Connections

c. connect to server dc2.adatum.com

d. roles

e. quit

f. metadata cleanup

Answer area:

1..

2..

3..

4..

5..

ANSWERS AND EXPLANATIONS

1) Answer: B. No

Explanation:

The proposed solution does not meet the goal. In Active Directory Domains and Trusts, the Operations Master option does not display the PDC emulator role. To find out which server holds the PDC emulator role, you should use the Active Directory Users and Computers snap-in or the Active Directory Schema snap-in.

Here is the correct procedure using Active Directory Users and Computers:

Open Active Directory Users and Computers.

Right-click the domain name (e.g., contoso.com) and select "Operations Masters."

In the Operations Masters window, click the "PDC" tab to see the server that holds the PDC emulator role.

Alternatively, you can use the command line tool netdom query fsmo to list all FSMO role holders, including the PDC emulator.

2) Answer: A. Yes

Explanation:

Running the command netdom.exe query fsmo at a command prompt lists all the FSMO (Flexible Single Master Operations) role holders in the domain, including the PDC (Primary Domain Controller) emulator. Therefore, this solution effectively identifies which server is the PDC emulator for the domain.

3) Answer: B. Run the Microsoft Azure Active Directory Connect wizard and enable Password writeback.

Explanation:

To ensure that users who reset their passwords using Azure AD Self-Service Password Reset (SSPR) can use the new passwords for on-premises resources in the AD DS domain, you need to enable password writeback. Password writeback is a feature of Azure AD Connect that allows password changes in Azure AD to be written back to the on-premises AD DS.

By running the Microsoft Azure Active Directory Connect wizard and selecting the Password writeback option, you configure Azure AD Connect to synchronize password changes from Azure AD back to the on-premises AD DS, ensuring that users can use their new passwords across both environments.

Options A, C, and D do not directly address the requirement to synchronize password changes from Azure AD to on-premises AD DS.

4) A. AAD DC Administrators is indeed the correct group.

Explanation:

The "AAD DC Administrators" group in Azure Active Directory Domain Services (Azure AD DS) has the necessary permissions to manage Group Policy Objects (GPOs). This group is specifically designed for managing Azure AD DS resources and aligns with the principle of least privilege for this task.

The other options provide broader permissions and are not as specific to managing GPOs alone.

Settings for user and computer objects in Azure Active Directory Domain Services (Azure AD DS) are often managed using Group Policy Objects (GPOs).

Azure AD DS includes built-in GPOs for the AADDC Users and AADDC Computers containers. You can customize these built-in GPOs to configure Group Policy as needed for your environment.

ANSWER (A): Members of the Azure AD DC administrators' group have "Group Policy administration privileges in the Azure AD DS domain, and can also create custom GPOs and organizational units (OUs). "

Reference:

https://docs.microsoft.com/en-us/azure/active-directory-domain-services/manage-group-policy

5) To ensure that the virtual machines can join Azure Active Directory Domain Services (Azure AD DS), follow these steps in the correct order:

Answer Area:

1. d. Create an Azure virtual network.

You need to create a virtual network to host both the Azure AD DS instance and the virtual machines.

2. e. Create an Azure AD DS instance.

Deploy Azure AD DS within the virtual network you created so that it is available for the virtual machines to join.

3. a. Modify the settings of the Azure virtual network.

Adjust the virtual network settings as necessary to ensure that the virtual machines can communicate with the Azure AD DS instance.

Explanation:

Create an Azure virtual network is the first step, as both Azure AD DS and the virtual machines need to reside within the same network to communicate.

Create an Azure AD DS instance comes next because you need to deploy the domain services within the virtual network.

Modify the settings of the Azure virtual network is the final step, as you need to ensure that network configurations allow the virtual machines to connect to the Azure AD DS instance.

Options b, c, and f are not required for joining Azure virtual machines to Azure AD DS. The Active Directory Domain Services role and Azure AD Connect are more relevant for on-premises environments or hybrid setups, and the Active Directory Domain Services Installation Wizard is used for on-premises AD installations, not for Azure AD DS.

Reference:

https://docs.microsoft.com/en-us/azure/active-directory-domain-services/tutorial-create-instance

6) Answer Area:

1. Add Admin1 to the following group:

a. AAD DC Administrators

2. Instruct Admin1 to apply the custom Group Policy settings by:

b. Modifying AADDC Computers GPO

Explanation:

Add Admin1 to the AAD DC Administrators group: Members of this group have the necessary permissions to manage Group Policy Objects (GPOs) in Azure AD DS, including creating and modifying GPOs. This group provides the appropriate level of privilege for GPO management in Azure AD DS.

Instruct Admin1 to modify the AADDC Computers GPO: This specific GPO is designed for managing settings related to computers in Azure AD DS. Modifying this GPO allows Admin1 to deploy custom settings to all computers in the domain, which is a targeted way to manage GPOs without affecting other default or broader GPOs.

Reference:

https://docs.microsoft.com/en-us/azure/active-directory-domain-services/manage-group-policy

The GPO can be linked on UO not to the domain

7) Answer Area:

b. Create a site and a subnet.

d. Pre-create an RODC account.

a. Instruct User1 to run the Active Directory Domain Services installation Wizard on Server1.

Explanation:

Create a site and a subnet: First, you need to create a new site named RemoteSite1 and assign the appropriate subnet to it. This step is necessary to ensure that Server1 is correctly identified as being in the new site, which will help in controlling replication and defining network topology.

Pre-create an RODC account: Before you can install the RODC, you must pre-create an RODC account in Active Directory. This step is required for the RODC installation process and ensures that you can manage the RODC's properties and permissions properly.

Instruct User1 to run the Active Directory Domain Services installation Wizard on Server1: After setting up the site and pre-creating the RODC account, you can instruct User1 to use the Active Directory Domain Services installation Wizard to install the RODC. User1 will need to perform this installation, but ensure that User1 has the required permissions to do so (usually granted by being a member of a specific AD group, not just local Administrators).

Note: Adding User1 to the Contoso\Administrators group is not necessary if User1 is not intended to perform the installation directly but instead needs specific delegated permissions. Creating a site link is not needed at this stage for the RODC deployment.

8) Answer: B. Operating System

Explanation:

To ensure that the Group Policy preferences in GPO1 apply

only to domain member servers and not to domain controllers or client computers, you can use Operating System item-level targeting.

Here's why:

Operating System item-level targeting allows you to apply Group Policy preferences based on the type of operating system. By configuring item-level targeting to apply only to servers (which typically run server operating systems), you can exclude domain controllers and client computers, which have different operating systems.

Other options:

A. Domain: These targets policies based on domain membership, but it does not differentiate between domain controllers, member servers, and client computers.

C. Security Group: This could be used if you have specific security groups that include only the member servers, but managing and maintaining security groups for this purpose might involve more administrative effort compared to using OS-based targeting.

D. Environment Variable: This is less suitable for distinguishing between types of computers (domain controllers vs. member servers vs. client computers) and might require more complex configurations.

Using Operating System targeting minimizes administrative effort and directly addresses the need to apply settings based on the type of computer.

9) Correct answers are:

c. Create two additional sites named Site2 and Site3. Move DC2 to Site2 and DC3 to Site3.

This step ensures that each domain controller is in a separate site. You need to create and assign the domain controllers to their respective sites.

b. Create an additional site link that contains Site1 and Site2.

This action sets up a site link between Site1 (DC1) and Site2 (DC2), allowing you to control the replication schedule between these sites independently.

e. Remove Site2 from DEFAULTIPSITELINK.

Removing Site2 from the default site link (DEFAULTIPSITELINK) ensures that replication between Site2 and other sites is controlled by the newly created site links rather than the default one.

Explanation:

Creating additional sites and moving domain controllers ensures proper segmentation.

Creating a site link allows control over the replication schedule.

Removing a site from DEFAULTIPSITELINK ensures that only the intended site links control replication between sites, minimizing interruptions and conflicts.

10) Correct answer: A. DC1

Initial replication and connectivity requirements

This FSMO role holder is only active when the role owner has inbounded replicated the configuration NC successfully since the Directory Service started.

Domain members of the forest only contact the FSMO role holder when they update the cross-references. DCs contact the

FSMO role holder when:

Domains are added or removed in the forest.

New instances of application directory partitions on DCs are added. For example, a DNS server has been enlisted for the default DNS application directory partitions.

Reference:

https://docs.microsoft.com/en-us/troubleshoot/windows-server/identity/fsmo-roles#domain%20naming

11) Answer: A. Select the Configure Hybrid Azure AD join option.

Hybrid Azure AD join needs to be configured to enable Computer1 to be used in Conditional Access Policies. Synchronized users, universal groups and domain local groups can be used in Conditional Access Policies.

Explanation:

To ensure that all objects, including devices and groups, can be used in Conditional Access policies after syncing your on-premises Active Directory domain with Azure Active Directory (Azure AD), you should:

Select the Configure Hybrid Azure AD join option: This option ensures that your on-premises devices are properly registered with Azure AD, which is crucial for Conditional Access policies that depend on device compliance and user sign-ins.

Clarification on Other Options:

B. Change the scope of Group1 and Group2 to Global: This might not be necessary unless there are specific issues with group scope impacting Azure AD synchronization.

C. Clear the Configure device writeback option: This action impacts the ability to write back device objects from Azure AD to on-premises AD and is not directly related to enabling Conditional Access.

D. Change the scope of Group2 to Universal: While changing group scopes can affect synchronization and policy application, the Hybrid Azure AD join option is more directly related to ensuring all objects, including devices, are properly handled in Conditional Access.

Using the Hybrid Azure AD join option helps with the synchronization and registration of devices, ensuring they are correctly managed by Conditional Access policies.

Reference:

https://learn.microsoft.com/en-us/azure/active-directory/conditional-access/howto-conditional-access-policy-compliant-device

12) Answer: D. For each site link, modify the options attribute.

Explanation:

Modifying the options attribute for each site link can indeed affect the replication behavior and efficiency in a multi-site Active Directory environment. Specifically:

Site Link Options: By setting specific options on site links, such as enabling or disabling certain features (like compression or notifications), you can optimize how replication occurs between sites. This can help reduce the convergence time by ensuring replication is more efficient and effective.

Comparison to Other Options:

A. Modify the replication schedule: Changes to the replication schedule control when replication occurs but do not impact the efficiency of replication paths directly.

B. Modify the site link costs: While changing site link costs affects the preferred path for replication, it doesn't necessarily improve the convergence time across all site links.

C. Create a site link bridge: Although creating a site link bridge can help with replication paths, modifying the site link options is a more direct way to fine-tune the replication behavior and improve convergence time.

By adjusting the options attribute of site links, you can control various aspects of replication, potentially leading to reduced convergence times and more efficient updates.

When you configure manual site link replication schedule is already setup to 15-minute replication cycle you cannot lower more down. so only option left is to change link site option attribute for use notify setting.

13) To configure a Network Load Balancing (NLB) cluster to authenticate using a group managed service account (gMSA), you need to perform the following steps in sequence:

Create a Key Distribution Service (KDS) root key: This step is required to enable the creation of gMSAs in the domain.

Create the gMSA: After enabling the KDS root key, you can create the gMSA.

Install the gMSA on the NLB cluster nodes: Finally, you need to install the gMSA on the servers where the NLB service is running.

Correct Order:

1. e. Add-KdsRootKey

This cmdlet creates a KDS root key required for the creation of gMSAs.

2. a. New-ADServiceAccount

This cmdlet creates the gMSA.

3. b. Install-ADServiceAccount

This cmdlet installs the gMSA on the servers, allowing them to use it for authentication.

Explanation:

Add-KdsRootKey: You need to create a KDS root key before you can create a gMSA. This key is used to encrypt the passwords of the gMSAs.

New-ADServiceAccount: After the KDS root key is available, you can create the gMSA using this cmdlet.

Install-ADServiceAccount: This cmdlet installs the gMSA on the server so that it can be used by services running on that server, including NLB.

Cmdlets not used in this sequence:

b. Install-ADServiceAccount: This cmdlet is used to install the gMSA on the servers, so it is used after creating the gMSA.

c. Add-ADComputerServiceAccount: This cmdlet adds the gMSA to specific computers, but you don't need this if you're installing the gMSA directly.

d. Set-KdsConfiguration: This cmdlet is used to configure KDS settings but is not required in this context.

f. Add-ADGroupMember: This cmdlet is used to add members to an AD group and is not relevant to gMSA creation or installation.

So, the correct sequence of cmdlets is:

1. e. Add-KdsRootKey

2. a. New-ADServiceAccount

3. b. Install-ADServiceAccount

14) Answer: A. Device writeback

Explanation:

To enable Windows Hello for Business on hybrid-joined devices, the Device writeback feature in Azure AD Connect is essential.

Here's why:

Device writeback: This feature allows devices that are registered in Azure AD to be written back to the on-premises AD. This ensures that the device identity and its associated attributes are synchronized back to the on-premises AD, which is necessary for enabling Windows Hello for Business on those devices. Without device writeback, the on-premises AD would not be aware of the Azure AD-registered devices, which could prevent proper functioning of Windows Hello for Business.

Clarification of Other Options:

B. Group writeback: This feature is used to write back Azure AD groups to the on-premises AD but is not related to device management or Windows Hello for Business.

C. Azure AD app and attribute filtering: This feature allows you to filter out which Azure AD apps and attributes are synchronized but does not affect device synchronization or Windows Hello for Business.

D. Password writeback: This feature allows users to reset their passwords in Azure AD and have those changes written back to the on-premises AD. It does not impact the device synchronization required for Windows Hello for Business.

E. Directory extension attribute sync: This feature allows you to synchronize additional attributes from AD to Azure AD but does not affect device writeback.

Thus, enabling Device writeback ensures that the necessary device information is synchronized between Azure AD and on-premises AD, allowing Windows Hello for Business to function correctly.

Reference:

https://docs.microsoft.com/en-us/windows/security/identity-protection/hello-for-business/hello-hybrid-cert-trust-prereqs

15) Correct answers are:

Admin1: b. Contoso\Domain Admins

Admin2: e. East Domain Admins

Explanation:

Admin1: b. Contoso\Domain Admins

Reasoning: Admin1 needs to create and manage Active Directory sites, which is a domain-level task. The Domain Admins group in the contoso.com domain has the necessary permissions to manage domain settings, including the creation and management of sites. Admin1 does not need forest-wide permissions, so membership in the Domain Admins group of the contoso.com domain is sufficient.

Admin2: e. East Domain Admins

Reasoning: Admin2 needs to deploy domain controllers in the east.contoso.com domain. The East Domain Admins group has the appropriate domain-level permissions required for managing domain controllers in the east.contoso.com domain.

Summary:

Contoso\Domain Admins is appropriate for tasks within the contoso.com domain, including site management.

East Domain Admins is suitable for domain-specific tasks in the east.contoso.com domain, including deploying domain controllers.

Membership in the Enterprise Admins group in the forest or the Domain Admins group in the forest root domain.

16) Answer: B. No

Explanation:

The Try Next Closest Site Group Policy Object (GPO) setting is used to determine whether clients should attempt to authenticate with domain controllers in a different site if the domain controllers in their current site are unavailable. It does not control or prioritize the authentication of clients to domain controllers in a specific site.

To ensure that client computers in the new branch office are primarily authenticated by the domain controllers in Site1, you should use Site Links and Site Link Costs to influence the selection of domain controllers.

Here's why:

Site Links and Costs: By adjusting the site link costs in Active Directory Sites and Services, you can influence which domain controllers are preferred for authentication. Lower costs make the site more preferred for authentication. You would set a lower cost for Site1's link to ensure it is the preferred site for authentication.

Site Placement: Ensure that the client computers in the new branch office are placed in a site configuration that links them to Site1 or adjust site link costs to make Site1 the preferred site for authentication.

The GPO setting you mentioned affects what happens if a domain controller in the client's current site is unavailable, not which site is preferred for authentication under normal circumstances.

17) Answer: B. No

Explanation:

Creating a new site (Site4) and adding it to the DEFAULTIPSITELINK will not ensure that client computers in the new branch office are primarily authenticated by the domain controllers in Site1. This action alone does not prioritize Site1 for client authentication.

To ensure client computers in the new branch office are primarily authenticated by domain controllers in Site1, you should:

Configure Site Link Costs: Adjust the costs of the site links in Active Directory Sites and Services. Lower the cost for the link between Site1 and the new branch office site (Site4) to make Site1 the preferred site for authentication.

EXAM AZ-800: ADMINISTERING WINDOWS SERVER HYBRID CORE INFRAST...

Place the New Branch Office in the Correct Site: Make sure that the new branch office's site (Site4) is correctly configured in Active Directory Sites and Services to reflect its physical location and connectivity.

By adjusting the site link costs, you can influence which site is preferred for authentication. The creation of a new site and adding it to DEFAULTIPSITELINK does not directly address the preference for authentication without modifying link costs or site configurations.

18) Answer: B. No

Explanation:

The Try Next Closest Site Group Policy Object (GPO) setting is designed to direct clients to attempt authentication with domain controllers in other sites if those in their current site are unavailable. It does not control or prioritize which domain controllers a client should use under normal circumstances.

To ensure that client computers in the new branch office are primarily authenticated by domain controllers in Site1, you should use a different approach, such as:

Adjusting Site Link Costs: Modify the site link costs in Active Directory Sites and Services. Lower the cost for the link between Site1 and the new branch office site to make Site1 the preferred site for authentication.

Proper Site Configuration: Ensure that the new branch office is assigned to a site that has Site1 as the primary or preferred site for client authentication by configuring site link costs appropriately.

The Try Next Closest Site setting will not affect primary authentication preferences, only fallback behavior if the preferred domain controllers are unavailable.

Extra explanation:

Configuring the Try Next Closest Site Group Policy Object (GPO) setting in a GPO that is linked to Site1 will not ensure that the client computers in the new office are primarily authenticated by the domain controllers in Site1.

The Try Next Closest Site GPO setting controls how a client computer attempts to locate a domain controller if it is unable to locate one in its own site. It causes the client to try to find a domain controller in the next closest site, rather than trying to authenticate with a domain controller in a remote site.

To achieve the goal of ensuring that the client computers in the new office are primarily authenticated by the domain controllers in Site1, you would need to configure the site link and site link costs between Site1 and the new office site so that the new office site has a higher cost to communicate with other sites than Site1. This way, the clients will prefer to authenticate with the domain controllers in Site1.

19) Answer: B. No

Explanation:

Right-clicking Default-First-Site-Name in Active Directory Sites and Services and selecting Properties will not provide information about which server is the PDC emulator for the domain.

To identify the PDC emulator:

Use the netdom command: Run netdom query fsmo from a command prompt. This command lists the FSMO role holders, including the PDC emulator.

Use Active Directory Users and Computers: Open the Active Directory Users and Computers console, right-click the domain, select "Operations Masters," and check the PDC tab to see the PDC emulator.

Use PowerShell: Execute the PowerShell command Get-ADDomain and look for the PDCEmulator property.

These methods directly provide the information about the PDC emulator, unlike checking the properties of the site in Active Directory Sites and Services.

20) To create, configure, and install a group managed service account (gMSA) for the new application, follow these steps:

Create the gMSA on a domain controller:

B. On DC1, run the New-ADServiceAccount cmdlet.

This cmdlet creates a new gMSA in Active Directory. It allows you to define the account and its properties.

Install the gMSA on the server where the application will use it:

C. On Server1, run the Install-ADServiceAccount cmdlet.

This cmdlet installs the gMSA on the server, making it available for use by services and applications.

Explanation:

A. On Server1, run the setspn command: This command is used to set Service Principal Names (SPNs) for an account, which is not required for creating or installing a gMSA.

D. On Server1, run the Get-ADServiceAccount cmdlet: This cmdlet is used to retrieve information about an existing gMSA, not for creating or installing it.

E. On DC1, run the Set-ADComputer cmdlet: This cmdlet is used to configure attributes of computer accounts, not specifically for gMSAs.

F. On DC1, run the Install-ADServiceAccount cmdlet: This cmdlet is incorrect because it should be run on the server where the gMSA will be used, not on the domain controller.

Therefore, the correct actions are:

B. On DC1, run the New-ADServiceAccount cmdlet.

C. On Server1, run the Install-ADServiceAccount cmdlet.

21) Let's analyze the statements about the Active Directory Forest structure and user/group membership:

Statement 1: You can add User1 to Group1

Yes. User1 belongs to the contoso.com domain, and Group1 is also in the same domain. Users within a domain can be added to domain local groups.

Statement 2: You can add User2 to Group3

No. User2 belongs to the fabrikam.com domain, and Group3 is in the adatum.com domain. By default, users cannot be added to groups across different domains within a forest.

Statement 3: You can grant Group2 permissions to the resources in the fabrikam.com domain

No. Group2 is a domain local group in the contoso.com domain. Domain local groups don't have permissions outside their own domain. They cannot be assigned permissions to resources in another domain (fabrikam.com) within the forest.

Explanation:

The Active Directory Forest structure creates a security boundary between domains. By default, resources and groups are isolated within their respective domains. To manage access across domains, you would need to configure trust relationships between the domains or use Universal groups which can span domains.

This is about trust.

Contoso <-> Adatum <-> Fabrikam

User1 is from Contoso

Group1 is from Adatum

Both forests trusted each other, so Yes.

User2 is from Fabrikam

Group2 is from Contoso

Both forests don't trust each other, so No.

Transitive trust is only applicable to domain under the said forest.

Group2 is from Contoso

Fabrikam is another forest

Both forests don't trust each other, so No.

Transitive trust is only applicable to domain under the said forest.

22) Correct Answer:

C. Enable Selective Authentication for the trust.

Explanation:

Enabling Selective Authentication allows you to control which users or groups from the trusted domain can authenticate to the resources in the trusting domain. After enabling Selective Authentication, you can then configure permissions to restrict authentication to members of fabrikam\Group1.

To ensure that only members of the group fabrikam\Group1 can authenticate to server1.contoso.com, you need to configure the forest trust to control which users from the fabrikam.com forest are allowed to authenticate.

Here's the correct approach:

Selective Authentication: You should enable Selective Authentication for the forest trust. This allows you to control which users or groups from the trusted domain can authenticate to resources in the trusting domain. By enabling Selective Authentication, you can then specify that only fabrikam \Group1 is allowed to authenticate to server1.contoso.com.

Explanation of Other Options:

A. Add fabrikam\Group1 to the local Users group on server1.contoso.com: This would allow fabrikam\Group1 users to log in if they were authenticated, but it does not control the authentication permission at the trust level.

B. Enable SID filtering for the trust: SID filtering protects against potential security risks by ensuring that SIDs from the trusted domain are not used to gain access to resources in the trusting domain. However, this doesn't specifically restrict authentication to fabrikam\Group1.

EXAM AZ-800: ADMINISTERING WINDOWS SERVER HYBRID CORE INFRAST...

D. Change the trust to a one-way external trust: This change would make the trust one-way and not suitable for scenarios where you want to allow authentication from the trusted domain.

Reference:

https://docs.microsoft.com/en-us/previous-versions/windows/it-pro/windows-server-2003/cc755321(v=ws.10)

23) The correct answer is:

D. DC1 and Server1 only.

In Active Directory, adding a user to the Backup Operators group grants that user the ability to back up files on servers within the domain where the group is located. Here's the breakdown of what User1 can do based on the scenario:

Backup Operators Group Scope: The Backup Operators group in Active Directory applies to the domain where the group is created. Therefore, User1 will have backup rights on servers within the contoso.com domain only.

Servers in Contoso.com: The servers that User1 can back up would be those located in the contoso.com domain.

Given that:

DC1 and Server1 are located in the contoso.com domain.

DC2 and Server2 are not explicitly mentioned as being in contoso.com, but typically, if not stated otherwise, they are assumed to be in the other domain (east.contoso.com).

Therefore, User1 can back up:

DC1 and Server1 (since these servers are in the contoso.com domain).

Members of the Backup Operators group can back up and restore all files on A computer, regardless of the permissions that protect those files.

This doesn't mean that the member of Backup operators' group can backup any computer and not just a Domain controller.

They do have the permissions needed to replace files (including operating system files) on domain controllers. Because members of this group can replace files on domain controllers, they're considered service administrators.

24) The correct configuration for setting up a password policy for local user accounts on Azure virtual machines joined to Azure Active Directory Domain Services (Azure AD DS) should be:

Sign in by using a user account that is a member of the:

1. a. AAD DC Administrators group

Use a Group Policy Object (GPO) linked to the:

2. a. AADDC Computers organizational unit (OU)

Explanation:

AAD DC Administrators Group: Members of this group have the necessary permissions to manage Group Policy Objects (GPOs) and make changes in Azure AD DS.

AADDC Computers Organizational Unit (OU): The password policy should be linked to the AADDC Computers OU, which applies to the Azure virtual machines that are members of the Azure AD DS domain. This OU contains all the computer objects in the domain, making it the correct scope for applying policies affecting these machines.

Summary:

Use a member of the AAD DC Administrators group to manage GPOs.

Link the GPO to the AADDC Computers OU to enforce the password policy.

25) To create a user named Admin1 in the domain contoso.com and grant Admin1 the ability to back up and restore files on SRV1 while adhering to the principle of least privilege, follow these steps:

Steps to Complete the Task:

Sign in to a Domain Controller:

Use a domain administrator account to sign in to a domain controller or a computer with administrative privileges to manage Active Directory.

Create the User Account (Admin1):

Open Active Directory Users and Computers.

Navigate to the appropriate Organizational Unit (OU) where you want to create the user.

Right-click the OU and select New > User.

Enter the details for the new user (Admin1), and follow the prompts to create the account.

Grant Backup and Restore Permissions on SRV1:

Sign in to SRV1 with an account that has administrative privileges.

Open Computer Management > Local Users and Groups > Groups.

Double-click the Backup Operators group and add the user Admin1 to this group. Members of the Backup Operators group can back up and restore files.

Verify Permissions:

Ensure Admin1 has the appropriate permissions to back up and restore files by checking the group membership and testing the functionality.

Explanation:

Creating the User: The user Admin1 needs to be created in Active Directory to have an account in the domain.

Granting Permissions: Adding Admin1 to the Backup Operators group on SRV1 ensures that Admin1 has the necessary permissions to back up and restore files. The Backup Operators group is designed to give users the capability to perform backup and restore operations without granting full administrative rights.

Summary:

Sign in to a domain controller to create Admin1 in Active Directory.

Sign in to SRV1 to add Admin1 to the Backup Operators group.

This approach follows the principle of least privilege by only granting the necessary permissions required for Admin1 to perform backup and restore tasks without giving broader administrative rights.

26) To ensure that the minimum password length for members of the BranchAdmins group is 12 characters, and that this change affects only the BranchAdmins group, follow these steps:

Sign in to a Domain Controller:

Log in to a domain controller or a computer with administrative privileges to manage Group Policy.

Create a New Group Policy Object (GPO):

Open the Group Policy Management Console (GPMC).

Navigate to the appropriate Organizational Unit (OU) where the BranchAdmins group is located or create a new GPO if necessary.

Right-click and select Create a GPO in this domain, and link it here.

Edit the GPO to Configure the Password Policy:

Right-click the newly created GPO and select Edit.

Go to Computer Configuration > Policies > Windows Settings > Security Settings > Account Policies > Password Policy.

Set the Minimum password length to 12 characters.

Apply the GPO to the BranchAdmins Group:

In the Group Policy Management Console, right-click the GPO and select Edit.

Navigate to Security Filtering on the Scope tab.

Remove Authenticated Users from the security filtering list.

Click Add, and add the BranchAdmins group.

Verify the Policy Application:

Ensure that the GPO is correctly linked and applied to the BranchAdmins group. Use the gpupdate command on affected computers or use Group Policy Results to verify.

Summary:

Sign in to a domain controller to manage Group Policy.

Create and configure a GPO to set the minimum password length.

Apply the GPO specifically to the BranchAdmins group to ensure the policy affects only its members.

27) To configure a Group Policy preference that places a shortcut to the folder \\srv1.contoso.com\data on the desktop of users in the Server Admins organizational unit (OU), follow these steps:

Log In to a Domain Controller or Management Computer:

Sign in with an account that has the necessary administrative privileges to manage Group Policy.

Open the Group Policy Management Console (GPMC):

Launch Group Policy Management from the Administrative Tools or start menu.

Create or Edit a Group Policy Object (GPO):

Locate the organizational unit (OU) named Server Admins in the GPMC.

Right-click the OU and select Create a GPO in this domain, and link it here if creating a new GPO, or choose an existing GPO to edit.

Edit the GPO to Add the Shortcut:

Right-click the GPO and select Edit.

Navigate to User Configuration > Preferences > Windows Settings > Shortcuts.

Right-click on the right pane, select New > Shortcut.

Set the Action to Create.

In the Target Path field, enter \\srv1.contoso.com\data.

In the Location field, choose Desktop.

Configure other settings as needed (such as the shortcut name).

Apply the GPO:

Close the GPO editor and ensure the GPO is linked to the Server Admins OU.

This configuration ensures that when users in the Server Admins OU log in to their computers, they will have a desktop shortcut to the specified folder.

28) To ensure that the domain controller DC3, located in the Seattle site, only replicates with DC1 and DC2 between 8 PM and 6 AM, follow these steps:

Log In to a Domain Controller or Management Computer:

Sign in with an account that has the required administrative privileges to manage Active Directory replication.

Open the Active Directory Sites and Services Console:

Launch Active Directory Sites and Services from the Administrative Tools or start menu.

Configure the Replication Schedule:

Navigate to Sites and locate the site where DC3 is located.

Expand the site and select Servers.

Click on DC3 and then on NTDS Settings.

Right-click the connection objects for DC1 and DC2 and select Properties.

Go to the Schedule tab and configure the replication schedule to allow replication only between 8 PM and 6 AM.

Apply and Confirm the Configuration:

Save the changes and ensure that the replication settings are correctly applied.

This setup ensures that DC3 will only replicate data with DC1 and DC2 during the specified hours.

29) To ensure that DC2 is the schema master for contoso.com, follow these steps:

Log In to a Domain Controller or Management Computer

Sign in with an account that has the required administrative privileges to manage Active Directory schema roles.

Open the Active Directory Schema Management Console:

On a Windows Server 2016/2019/2022 machine:

If the Active Directory Schema snap-in is not already installed, install it by running the following command in an elevated Command Prompt:

regsvr32 schmmgmt.dll

Then, open Microsoft Management Console (MMC), and add the Active Directory Schema snap-in:

Run mmc.exe.

Go to File > Add/Remove Snap-in.

Select Active Directory Schema, then click Add and OK.

Transfer the Schema Master Role:

In the Active Directory Schema console, right-click on Active Directory Schema and select Operations Master.

Click on Change to transfer the schema master role to DC2.

Confirm the action and ensure the role has been transferred successfully.

Verify the Schema Master Role:

Confirm that DC2 is now listed as the schema master in the Operations Master window.

By completing these steps, DC2 will be set as the schema master for contoso.com.

30) Correct answer: D. ntdsutil.exe

To create a custom Active Directory partition for a DNS zone and ensure it replicates to specific domain controllers, you should use the ntdsutil.exe tool.

Explanation:

A. Windows Admin Center: This is a management tool for various Windows Server features, but it does not handle the creation of custom Active Directory partitions.

B. DNS Manager: This tool is used to manage DNS zones and records but does not manage Active Directory partitions.

C. Active Directory Sites and Services: This tool is used for managing sites and replication topology but does not create or manage custom Active Directory partitions.

D. ntdsutil.exe: This command-line tool is specifically used for various Active Directory database management tasks, including creating custom Active Directory partitions and managing their replication.

Thus, the correct answer is D. ntdsutil.exe.

31) To deploy the RODC on Server1 while ensuring compliance with the principle of least privilege and meeting the specified requirements, you should follow these steps:

1. b. Create a site and a subnet.

2. d. Pre-create an RODC account.

3. a. Instruct User1 to run the Active Directory Domain Services Installation Wizard on Server1.

Explanation:

Create a site and a subnet (b):

This ensures that Server1 will be correctly placed in the new site named RemoteSite1.

Pre-create an RODC account (d):

This allows you to delegate the installation and configuration permissions to User1 without giving them broader administrative rights.

Instruct User1 to run the Active Directory Domain Services Installation Wizard on Server1 (a):

After the RODC account is pre-created, User1 can proceed with the installation on Server1, utilizing the delegated permissions.

Summary:

Create a site and a subnet.

Pre-create an RODC account.

Instruct User1 to run the Active Directory Domain Services Installation Wizard on Server1.

32) Correct answer: A. Server3 only.

Based on the images and the information, Shortcut1 will be applied to

Here's why:

The image shows the Targeting Editor for a Group Policy Object (GPO) preference item.

The targeting item is configured to apply the preference only to computers where the operating system is Windows Server 2022 Family.

Out of the computers listed in the table (Computer1, Server1, Server2, and Server3), only Server3 runs Windows Server 2022.

Therefore, only Server3 meets the targeting criteria for Shortcut1 and will receive the shortcut preference.

33) The correct answer is:

C. For each site link, modify the options attribute.

Explanation:

Modifying the options attribute for each site link can enable Change Notification Replication, which reduces the replication latency by ensuring that changes are replicated as soon as they occur, rather than waiting for the next scheduled replication interval. This approach minimizes the delay in propagating changes across different sites in the AD DS forest.

In the Attribute Editor tab, double click on Options.

If the Value(s) box shows <not set>, type 1.

There is one caveat however. Change notification will fail with manual connection objects. If your connection objects are not created by the KCC the change notification setting is meaningless. If it's a manual connection object, it will NOT inherit the Options bit from the Site Link. Enjoy your 15-minute replication latency.

34) To meet the requirements specified, you should use the following group types:

1. Organize users: a. Domain global

2. Assign permissions: b. Domain local

Explanation:

Organize users (Domain global):

Domain global groups are used to organize users within a domain. In the contoso.com forest, you can use domain global groups to manage users across the various child domains (amer.contoso.com, apac.contoso.com, emea.contoso.com). This ensures that users are added directly to groups within their own forest.

Assign permissions (Domain local):

Domain local groups are used to assign permissions to resources within a domain. In the fabrikam.com forest, you can use domain local groups to assign permissions to resources. You can then use universal groups to add domain global groups from the contoso.com forest to the domain local groups in the fabrikam.com forest, leveraging the bidirectional trust to grant access.

Universal groups could be used to aggregate domain global groups from multiple domains, but they are not specifically required in this scenario if the goal is to minimize the number of groups and manage permissions effectively through domain local groups.

35) Correct answers:

1. User1 can be assigned permissions for Share3. (Yes)

-> There is an Outgoing trust, So we trust Adatum. Since this is forest trust, child domain, also can assign permissions to Adatum users.

2. User2 can be assigned permissions for Share1. (No)

-> Type trust is outgoint to Adatum. Only Adatum users can sign-in to Contoso forest.

User3 can be assigned permissions for Share1. (No)

-> Type trust is outgoint to Adatum. Only Adatum users can sign-in to Contoso forest.

SHARE3: EAST.CONTOSO

-> USER1: Adatum domain (OUTGOING TRUST) => GRANTED so TRUE

SHARE1: ADATUM.com

-> USER2: Contoso domain (NO TRUST) => ACCESS NOT GRANTED so FALSE

-> USER3: EAST.Contoso domain (OUTGOING TRUST) => NOT GRANDED so FALSE

Since Share3 trusts User1, so User1 can assign permission for Share3. As per Microsoft: "A one-way trust is a unidirectional authentication path created between two domains (trust flows in one direction, and access flows in the other). This means that in a one-way trust between a trusted domain and a trusting domain, users or computers in the trusted domain can access resources in the trusting domain. However, users in the trusting domain cannot access resources in the trusted domain. Some one-way trusts can be either nontransitive or transitive, depending on the type of trust being created."

Reference:

https://learn.microsoft.com/en-us/previous-versions/windows/it-pro/windows-server-2003/cc759554(v=ws.10)?redirectedfrom=MSDN

36) Based on the information and the image, here's the answer:

1. Name:

b. PolicyDefinitions

2. Server:

d. DC1 and DC2 only

Explanation:

The image doesn't contain specific information about the servers. However, best practices for managing Group Policy Central Stores in Active Directory recommend creating the Central Store on any Domain Controller (DC) in the domain.

Since this scenario deals with a Forest (contoso.com) containing a child domain (east.contoso.com), it's ideal to create the Central Store on Domain Controllers in both the parent and child domain for better accessibility and replication across the forest.

PolicyDefinitions is the standard naming convention for the Central Store folder.

Therefore, to manage Group Policy template files for the entire forest (contoso.com and east.contoso.com), create a folder named PolicyDefinitions on any Domain Controller (DC1 or DC2) but not on member servers (Server1).

37) To configure DC3 as the authoritative time server for the domain, follow these options:

1. Role: c. PDC emulator

2. Console: d. Active Directory Users and Computers

Explanation:

PDC emulator role (c):

The PDC emulator is responsible for domain time synchronization and acts as the authoritative time source in the domain.

Active Directory Users and Computers console (d):

Although the PDC emulator role can be managed through the Active Directory Domains and Trusts console, it is more commonly transferred using the Active Directory Users and Computers console. You can access the Operations Masters role transfer options from the "Operations Masters" section in the console.

Therefore, to set DC3 as the authoritative time server, transfer the PDC emulator role using the Active Directory Users and Computers console.

38) The correct sequence for ensuring that Windows containers on Server1 can authenticate with the contoso.com domain is:

1. d. In contoso.com, create a gMSA and a standard user account.

2. e. From a domain-joined computer, create a credential spec file and copy the file to Server1.

3. a. On Server1, install and run ccg.exe.

Explanation:

Create a gMSA and a standard user account (d):

First, create the group managed service account (gMSA) and a standard user account in the contoso.com domain.

Create a credential spec file and copy it to Server1 (e):

On a domain-joined computer, create the credential spec file using the gMSA. This file contains the authentication details required for the containers. Copy this file to Server1.

Install and run ccg.exe (a):

On Server1, install and run the ccg.exe tool to configure the containers to use the credential spec file for authentication. This step configures the Windows containers to authenticate using the gMSA.

39) The best account type for Azure AD Connect cloud sync is:

B. Group Managed Service Account (gMSA)

Here's why:

System-assigned managed identity: This option is not suitable for on-premises accounts used by Azure AD Connect cloud sync. It's designed for Azure resources.

User account: While a user account might seem like a possibility, it's not recommended due to security concerns. User accounts can be compromised, and their passwords need to be managed.

InetOrgPerson: This is not a relevant account type for service accounts used with Azure AD Connect cloud sync.

Group Managed Service Account (gMSA):

A gMSA is a secure type of account specifically designed for running managed services on Windows Server.

It offers several benefits:

Security: Credentials are automatically managed and rotated by the operating system, reducing the risk of compromise.

Permissions: The gMSA automatically obtains the necessary permissions to access resources on domain controllers.

Scalability: A single gMSA can be used by multiple instances of Azure AD Connect cloud sync across different servers.

Therefore, a Group Managed Service Account (gMSA) is the most secure and efficient option for the Azure AD Connect cloud sync service account.

40) To ensure that if an attacker compromises the computer account of an RODC (Read-Only Domain Controller), they cannot view the Employee-Number AD DS attribute, you should

modify:

D. schema

Explanation:

Configuration (A): The configuration partition contains information about the configuration of the Active Directory environment, such as sites and services. It does not control attribute visibility or permissions.

Global catalog (B): The global catalog holds a partial replica of all objects in the forest, but it does not manage permissions or attribute visibility at the schema level.

Domain (C): The domain partition holds information about objects within the domain but does not directly manage how attributes are filtered or hidden from RODCs.

Schema (D): The schema partition defines the attributes and classes in Active Directory. By modifying the schema to set the Employee-Number attribute as sensitive or confidential, you can ensure that RODCs do not cache this attribute. This approach prevents sensitive information from being stored on RODCs, thus limiting the exposure of this attribute even if the RODC is compromised.

By adjusting the schema to ensure that certain attributes are not cached on RODCs, you help secure sensitive data.

41) Correct answers are:

1. User1 can use self-service password reset (SSPR) to reset his password. (Yes)

-> Password Write back is enabled.

2. If User1 connects to Microsoft Exchange Online, an on-

premises domain controller provides authentication. (Yes)

-> Pass-Through authentication is in use; therefore, AD is the Identity Provider.

3. You can add User2 to Group1 as a member. (No)

-> "User2" is under "OU2" which is not synced to the Azure Tenant.

User2 is in OU2, which is not selected for synchronization according to the provided configuration details. Since User2's OU is not included in the synchronization scope, you cannot directly add User2 to Group1 from the on-premises AD.

42) To synchronize your on-premises Active Directory Domain Services (AD DS) domain with an Azure AD tenant and enable password hash synchronization, you should:

1. Install: b. Azure AD Connect

2. Use: b. Azure AD Connect

Explanation:

Install (b. Azure AD Connect):

Azure AD Connect is the software required for synchronizing your on-premises AD DS domain with Azure AD. It handles both the synchronization of directory data and the configuration of password hash synchronization.

Use (b. Azure AD Connect):

Azure AD Connect is also the tool used to enable password hash synchronization. During the setup and configuration of Azure AD Connect, you can choose to enable password hash synchronization as part of the installation process.

43) Correct answers are:

User1:

If User1 is created in a domain, it will be replicated to all domain controllers within that domain. If DC1, DC2, and DC3 are domain controllers within the same domain, User1 should be replicated to all of them. However, if DC4 is in a different domain or forest, it would not receive this update.

Attribute1:

Schema changes, such as creating a new attribute, are replicated across all domain controllers in the forest. However, if DC4 is not in the same forest or does not receive schema updates for any reason, it would not have this attribute.

Answer:

User1:

c. DC2 and DC3 only (assuming DC4 is in a different domain or forest)

Attribute1:

c. DC2 and DC3 only (assuming DC4 is not part of the schema replication or forest)

Explanation:

User1: Replicated to domain controllers in the same domain. If DC4 is in a different domain or forest, User1 will not be replicated there.

Attribute1: Schema changes are normally replicated across all domain controllers in the forest, but if DC4 is outside the schema replication scope, it would not receive the attribute.

User1:

This is a domain-level object.

Since DC1 and DC2 are in the same domain (adatum.com), User1 will be replicated to DC2.

DC3 is in a different domain (west.adatum.com), but it is in the same forest. Since it's a Global Catalog (GC) server, it will receive a partial replica of the adatum.com domain, including the newly created User1.

DC4 is in a completely different forest (contoso.com) and there is no direct trust relationship between contoso.com and west.adatum.com, so User1 will not be replicated to DC4.

Attribute1:

This is a schema-level object. The schema is a forest-wide object.

The schema master for the adatum.com forest is DC1, so any changes to the schema (such as adding a new attribute) are initially made on DC1.

These changes are then replicated to all other domain controllers in the adatum.com forest, which includes DC2 and DC3.

However, DC4 is in a different forest, so it will not receive the schema changes made in the adatum.com forest.

In summary, User1 and Attribute1 will be replicated to DC2 and DC3

44) To configure Storage Replica for replicating a volume from Server1 to Server2, you should install Windows Admin Center on:

B. CLIENT1

Explanation:

Server1 (A): While you can manage and configure storage on Server1, it's not necessary to install Windows Admin Center directly on the server that is involved in the replication.

CLIENT1 (B): Windows Admin Center is typically installed on a management workstation or a dedicated management server, not directly on the servers involved in the replication. Installing it on CLIENT1 (a management workstation) allows you to manage multiple servers, including Server1 and Server2, from a single location.

DC1 (C): Installing Windows Admin Center on a domain controller is not recommended unless it's necessary. It is usually better to keep domain controllers focused on their primary role and use a separate management workstation or server for administration tasks.

Server2 (D): Similar to Server1, installing Windows Admin Center directly on Server2 is not necessary. It is better to use a management station or server for configuring and managing Storage Replica.

Summary:

Install Windows Admin Center on CLIENT1 to manage and configure Storage Replica for both Server1 and Server2.

45) Correct answer: A. Azure Active Directory admin center is indeed the correct tool for managing password policies in Azure AD, which includes implementing custom banned password policies.

Explanation:

Azure Active Directory admin center (A): In Azure AD, you can configure custom banned password lists and password policies, including preventing specific words like "contoso" from being used in passwords. Since Azure AD Connect syncs these policies with on-premises AD, configuring them in the Azure AD admin center ensures that the password policy is enforced across both Azure AD and the on-premises AD domain.

Active Directory Users and Computers (B): While this tool is used for managing user accounts and settings, specific password restrictions like banned passwords are typically managed through Azure AD if you are using Azure AD Connect.

Synchronization Service Manager (C): This tool manages the synchronization between AD DS and Azure AD but does not handle password policies.

Windows Admin Center (D): This tool is primarily for managing Windows Server environments and does not manage Azure AD password policies.

So, for managing custom banned passwords that sync with Azure AD, the Azure Active Directory admin center is indeed the right choice.

You can configure the custom banned password list, which includes preventing the use of the word "contoso" as part of passwords, through the Azure Active Directory admin center. This allows you to enforce password policies centrally for both on-premises AD DS domain and Azure AD users.

46) To create a custom Active Directory partition for storing a DNS zone and ensure that it replicates to only four specific domain controllers, you should use:

D. ntdsutil.exe

Explanation:

Windows Admin Center (A): This tool is used for managing Windows Server environments and provides a graphical interface for many administrative tasks but does not directly support creating custom AD partitions for DNS zones.

Set-DnsServer (B): This PowerShell cmdlet is used to configure DNS server settings but does not manage the creation of custom Active Directory partitions.

New-ADObject (C): This PowerShell cmdlet is used to create new AD objects but is not typically used for creating custom Active Directory partitions.

ntdsutil.exe (D): This command-line tool is specifically used for managing Active Directory, including creating and configuring custom Active Directory partitions. To store a DNS zone in a custom AD partition and control replication, you would use ntdsutil.exe to create the partition and configure replication settings as needed.

Summary:

Use ntdsutil.exe to create a custom Active Directory partition and manage its replication scope.

47) To create a group managed service account (gMSA) named Account1 and ensure that Group1 can use Account1, you should complete the script as follows:

Answer area:

(1) d. New-ADServiceAccount

(2) c. -

PrincipalsAllowedToDelegateToAccount

Explanation:

(1) New-ADServiceAccount (d):

The New-ADServiceAccount cmdlet is used to create a new group managed service account (gMSA) in Active Directory. This is the appropriate cmdlet for creating a gMSA.

(2) -PrincipalsAllowedToDelegateToAccount (c):

The -PrincipalsAllowedToDelegateToAccount parameter is used to specify which groups or users are allowed to use the gMSA. By setting this parameter, you can ensure that Group1 is allowed to use the gMSA Account1.

Summary:

Use New-ADServiceAccount to create the gMSA.

Use -PrincipalsAllowedToDelegateToAccount to specify the group that can use the gMSA.

49) When attempting to remove a custom application partition and the process fails, it is likely that the domain controller responsible for hosting the custom application partition is unavailable. The domain controller in question should be the one that holds the partition data.

Answer: C. DC3

Explanation:

Custom Application Partition: This type of partition is typically created to store application-specific data and is usually not replicated to all domain controllers by default. It is often hosted on specific domain controllers designated to manage that partition.

DC3 (C): If the removal of the custom application partition fails, it indicates that the domain controller which holds or is responsible for that partition is not available. In this scenario, DC3 is likely the one that holds the custom application partition, and its unavailability is preventing the successful removal of the partition.

DC1, DC2, DC4 (A, B, D): These domain controllers may not hold the custom application partition, so their availability status would not impact the removal process of this partition.

Summary:

The domain controller that is unavailable and causing the failure to remove the custom application partition is likely DC3.

50) Correct answer:

1. Roles

2. Connections

3. Connect to server dc2.adatum.com

4. quit

5. seize schema master

Reference:

https://learn.microsoft.com/en-us/troubleshoot/windows-server/identity/transfer-or-seize-operation-master-roles-in-ad-ds#seize-or-transfer-operation-master-roles

PRACTICE TEST II

1) Case Study

Company Information:

ADatum Corporation is a manufacturing company with its main office in Seattle and branch offices in Los Angeles and Montreal.

Fabrikam Partnership:

ADatum has recently partnered with Fabrikam, Inc., another manufacturing company with a main office in Boston and a branch office in Orlando. Both companies plan to collaborate on several joint projects.

Existing Environment:

ADatum AD DS Environment:

ADatum's on-premises network includes an Active Directory Domain Services (AD DS) forest named adatum.com. This forest consists of two domains: adatum.com and east.adatum.com. The domain controllers are listed in the following table.

Name	Domain	Operations master roles
DC1	adatum.com	Schema master
DC2	adatum.com	*None*
DC3	east.adatum.com	PDC emulator, RID master

Fabrikam AD DS Environment:

The on-premises network of Fabrikam contains an AD DS forest named fabrikam.com.

The forest contains two domains named fabrikam.com and south.fabrikam.com.

The fabrikam.com domain contains an organizational unit (OU) named Marketing.

Server Infrastructure:

The adatum.com domain contains the servers shown in the following table.

Name	Role
HyperV1	Hyper-V
SSPace1	File and Storage Services

HyperV1 contains the virtual machines shown in the following table.

Name	Operating system	Description
VM1	Windows Server 2022 Datacenter	Joined to the adatum.com domain Contains a file share named Data1 and a local user named User1
VM2	Red Hat Enterprise Linux (RHEL)	Contains a local user named User2
VM3	Windows Server 2022 Standard	Joined to the adatum.com domain Has the File and Storage Services role installed

All the virtual machines on HyperV1 have only the default management tools installed.

SSPace1 contains the Storage Spaces virtual disks shown in the following table.

Name	Number of physical disks	Redundancy
Disk1	8	Three-way mirror
Disk2	12	Parity

Azure Resources:

ADatum has an Azure subscription that contains an Azure AD tenant. Azure AD Connect is configured to sync the adatum.com forest with Azure AD.

The subscription contains the virtual networks shown in the following table.

Name	Location	Subnet
VNet1	West US	Subnet1, Subnet2
VNet2	West US	SubnetA, SubnetB

The subscription contains the Azure Private DNS zones shown in the following table.

Name	Virtual network link
Zone1.com	VNet1
Zone2.com	VNet2
Zone3.com	None

The subscription contains the virtual machines shown in the following table.

Name	Operating system	Security type
Server1	Windows Server 2022 Datacenter: Azure Edition	Trusted launch
Server2	Windows Server 2022 Datacenter: Azure Edition	Standard
Server3	Windows Server 2022 Datacenter	Standard
Server4	Windows Server 2019 Datacenter	Trusted launch

All the servers are in a workgroup.

The subscription contains a storage account named storage1 that has a file share named share1.

Requirements:

Planned Changes:

ADatum plans to implement the following changes:

• Sync Data1 to share1.

• Configure an Azure runbook named Task1.

• Enable Azure AD users to sign in to Server1.
• Create an Azure DNS Private Resolver that has the following configurations:

• Name: Private1

• Region: West US

• Virtual network: VNet1

• Inbound endpoint: SubnetB

• Enable users in the adatum.com domain to access the resources in the south.fabrikam.com domain.

Technical Requirements:

ADatum identifies the following technical requirements:
• **The data on SSPace1 must be available always.**
• **DC2 must become the schema master if DC1 fails.**

• **VM3 must be configured to enable per-folder quotas.**

• **Trusts must allow access to only the required resources.**

• **The users in the Marketing OU must have access to storage1.**

• **Azure Automanage must be used on all supported Azure virtual machines.**
• **A direct SSH session must be used to manage all the supported virtual machines on HyperV1.**

You need to ensure that access to storage1 for the Marketing OU users meets the technical requirements.

What should you implement?

A. Active Directory Federation Services (AD FS)

B. Azure AD Connect in staging mode

C. Azure AD Connect cloud sync

D. Azure AD Connect in active mode

2) Your network contains an Active Directory Domain Services (AD DS) domain.

To create a new user named User1 using Active Directory Administrative Center, which two attributes are mandatory?

A. Password

B. Profile path

C. User SamAccountName logon

D. Full name

E. First name

F. User UPN logon

3) Your on-premises network includes an Active Directory Domain Services (AD DS) domain. The domain comprises the following servers:

Name	Description
DC1	Domain naming master, PDC emulator, and RID master
DC2	Schema master and infrastructure master
RODC1	Read-only domain controller (RODC)
Server1	Azure AD Connect server
Server2	Azure AD Application Proxy connector

The domain controllers do not have internet access. You plan to implement Azure AD Password Protection for the domain and need to deploy Azure AD Password Protection agents. The solution must ensure that:

- **All Azure AD Password Protection policies are enforced.**
- **Agent updates are applied automatically.**
- **Administrative effort is minimized.**

What should you do?

Answer area:

Install the Azure AD Password Protection agent on:

a. DC1 only

b. DC1 and DC2 only

c. DC1, DC2, and RODC1

2. Install the Azure AD Password Protection Proxy on:

a. DC1

b. DC2

c. RODC1

d. Server1

e. Server2

4) Hotspot

Your on-premises network has a single-domain Active Directory Domain Services (AD DS) forest that syncs with an Azure AD tenant named contoso.com using Azure AD Connect. You need to ensure that users with a custom attribute labeled NoSync are excluded from synchronization.

How should you configure the Azure AD Connect cloudFiltered attribute, and which tool should you use?

To answer, choose the appropriate options in the answer area.

Answer area:

1. Attribute:

a. False

b. Null

c. True

2. Tool:

a. ADSI Edit

b. Synchronization Rules Editor

c. The Microsoft Azure AD Connect wizard

5) To fulfill the technical requirements for VM2, what action should you take?

A. Deploy shielded virtual machines.

B. Activate the Guest services integration service.

C. Implement Credential Guard.

D. Turn on enhanced session mode.

6) Your network has an Active Directory Domain Services (AD DS) domain with a user named User1. User1 belongs to a group called Group1 and is located in an organizational unit (OU) named OU1. The domain has configured minimum password lengths as indicated in the following table.

Value	Location
10	Default Domain Policy
12	Default Domain Controllers Policy
8	Group Policy linked to OU1
14	Password settings object applied to Group1
7	Password settings object applied to User1

What is the minimum password length that User1 should use when changing to a new password?

A. 7

B. 8

C. 10

D. 12

E. 14

7) SIMULATION

You need to create a Group Policy Object (GPO) named GPO1 that will apply exclusively to a group named MemberServers. To accomplish this, sign in to the necessary computer or computers.

8) Hotspot

You have 10 on-premises servers running Windows Server and plan to use the Azure Network Adapter to connect these servers to resources in Azure.

Which prerequisites do you require on-premises and in Azure?

Answer area:

1. To configure the on-premises servers, use:

a. Azure CLI

b. Routing and Remote Access

c. Server Manager

d. Windows Admin Center

2. To connect the Azure resources and Azure Network Server Manager Adapter, use:

a. Azure Bastion Azure Firewall

b. An Azure virtual network gateway

c. A private endpoint

d. A public Azure Load Balancer

9) Drag Drop

You have a server named Server1 with Windows Admin Center installed. The certificate used by Windows Admin Center, which was issued by a certification authority (CA), has expired. You need to replace this certificate.

Which three actions should you perform in sequence?

To answer, choose the appropriate actions (a to f) from the list of actions to the answer area and arrange them in the correct order (1, 2 and 3).

Select and Place:

Actions:

a. Obtain and install a new certificate.

b. From Internet Information Services (IIS) Manager, bind a certificate.

c. Run Windows Admin Center Setup and select Remove.

d. Run Windows Admin Center Setup and select Repair.

e. Run Windows Admin Center Setup and select Change.

f. Copy the certificate thumbprint.

Answer area:

1..

2..

3..

10) Hotspot

You have an on-premises server named Server1 running Windows Server with internet access, and you also have an Azure subscription. You need to set up monitoring for Server1 using Azure Monitor.

Which resources should you create in the subscription, and what should you install on Server1?

Answer area:

1. In the subscription, create:

a. An Azure Files storage account

b. A Log Analytics workspace

c. An Azure SQL database and a data collection rule

d. An Azure Blob Storage account and a data collection rule

2. On Server1, install:

a. The Azure Monitor agent

b. The Analytics gateway

c. The Device Health Attestation server role

11) You have an on-premises Active Directory Domain Services (AD DS) domain that syncs with an Azure Active Directory (Azure AD) tenant. The domain includes two servers, Server1 and Server2.

Admin1, a user, is part of the local Administrators group on both servers. You plan to manage Server1 and Server2 using Azure Arc, and the Azure Arc objects will be added to a resource group named RG1.

Your goal is to enable Admin1 to configure Server1 and Server2 for management through Azure Arc.

What is the first step you should take?

A. Generate a new onboarding script from the Azure portal.

B. Assign Admin1 the Azure Connected Machine Onboarding role for RG1.

C. Hybrid Azure AD join Server1 and Server2.

D. Create an Azure cloud-only account for Admin1.

12) Hotspot

Your network includes two Active Directory Domain Services (AD DS) forests, contoso.com and fabrikam.com, connected by a two-way forest trust. Each forest has a single domain. The domains contain the servers listed in the table below.

Name	Domain	Description
Server1	contoso.com	Hosts a Windows Admin Center gateway
Server2	fabrikam.com	Hosts resources that will be managed remotely by using Windows Admin Center on Server1

You need to set up resource-based constrained delegation to allow users in contoso.com to use Windows Admin Center on Server1 to connect to Server2.

How should you complete the command?

Answer area:

1. Set-ADComputer -Identity:

a. (Get-ADComputer server1.contoso.com)

b. (Get-ADComputer server2.fabrikam.com)

c. (Get-ADGroup 'Contoso\Domain Users')

d. (Get-ADGroup 'Fabrikam\Domain Users')

2. -PrincipalsAllowedToDelegateToAccount:

a. (Get-ADComputer server1.contoso.com)

b. (Get-ADComputer server2.fabrikam.com)

c. (Get ADGroup 'Contoso\Domain Users')

d. (Get-ADGroup 'Fabrikam\Domain Users')

13) Hotspot

You have a server named Server1 running Windows Server with the Hyper-V server role installed. You need to restrict which Hyper-V module cmdlets helpdesk users can use when administering Server1 remotely. You configure Just Enough Administration (JEA) and successfully create the role capabilities and session configuration files.

How should you complete the PowerShell command?

Answer area:

(1) -Path.\HyperVJeaConfig

(2) -Name 'HyperVJeaHelpDesk' -Force

(1) a. Enter-PSSession

  b. New-PSSessionConfiguration File

  c. Register-PSSessionConfiguration

(2) a. .ps1

  b. .psm1

  c. .psrc

  d. .pssc

14) You have an Azure virtual machine named VM1 running Windows Server and an Azure subscription with Microsoft Defender for Cloud enabled. To use the Azure Policy guest configuration feature to manage VM1, what should you do?

A. Add the PowerShell Desired State Configuration (DSC) extension to VM1.

B. Configure VM1 to use a user-assigned managed identity.

C. Configure VM1 to use a system-assigned managed identity.

D. Add the Custom Script Extension to VM1.

15) Hotspot

You have an Azure subscription called sub1 and 500 on-premises virtual machines running Windows Server.

You plan to onboard these virtual machines to Azure Arc by executing the Azure Arc deployment script.

To authenticate access to sub1, you need to create an identity for the script. The solution must adhere to the principle of least privilege.

How should you complete the command?

Answer area:

(1) -DisplayName 'Arc-for-servers' -Role **(2)**

(1) a. New-AzADAppCredential

    b. New-AzADServicePrincipal

    c. New-AzUserAssignedIdentity

(2) a. 'Azure Connected Machine Onboarding'

    b. 'Virtual Machine Contributor'

    c. 'Virtual Machine User Login'

16) You have an Azure virtual machine named VM1 with only a private IP address. You have set up the Windows Admin Center extension on VM1. You are using a Windows 11 computer for server management. To manage VM1 using Windows Admin Center from the Azure portal, you need to ensure the following configuration.

What should you configure?

A. an Azure Bastion host on the virtual network that contains VM1.

B. a VPN connection to the virtual network that contains VM1.

C. a private endpoint on the virtual network that contains VM1.

D. a network security group (NSG) rule that allows inbound traffic on port 443.

17) Your company has a main office and a branch office connected via a WAN link, with each office having a firewall that filters WAN traffic. The branch office network includes 10 Windows Server machines, all of which are managed exclusively from the main office. To manage these servers, you plan to use a Windows Admin Center gateway installed on a server in the branch office with default settings. You need to configure the branch office firewall to permit the necessary inbound connections to the Windows Admin Center gateway.

Which inbound TCP port should you allow?

A. 443

B. 3389

C. 5985

D. 6516

18) You have an Azure subscription with the following resources:

- An Azure Log Analytics workspace
- An Azure Automation account
- Azure Arc

You have onboarded an on-premises server named Server1 to Azure Arc. You need to manage Microsoft updates on Server1 using Azure Arc.

Which two actions should you perform?

A. From the Automation account, enable Update Management for Server1.

B. From the Virtual machines data source of the Log Analytics workspace, connect Server1.

C. On Server1, install the Azure Monitor agent.

D. Add Microsoft Sentinel to the Log Analytics workspace.

19) Hotspot

You have an on-premises Active Directory Domain Services (AD DS) domain that synchronizes with an Azure Active Directory (Azure AD) tenant. You have an on-premises web application named WebApp1 that supports only Kerberos authentication. To allow users to access WebApp1 using their Azure AD accounts while minimizing administrative effort, you need to implement a solution.

What should you configure?

Answer area:

1. In Azure AD:

a. The Azure AD Application Proxy connector

b. The Azure AD Application Proxy service

c. Web Application Proxy

2. On-premises:

a. The Azure AD Application Proxy connector

b. The Azure AD Application Proxy service

c. Web Application Proxy

20) SIMULATION

You need to collect errors from the System event log of SRV1 and send them to a Log Analytics workspace.

The necessary source files are located in a folder named \dc1.contoso.com\install.

To complete this task, sign in to the required computer or computers.

21) You have a server named Server1 running Windows Server with the DNS Server role installed. Server1 hosts a DNS zone named contoso.com. A partner company operates a DNS server named Server2, which hosts a DNS zone named fabrikam.com. To ensure that Server1 forwards all name resolution requests for fabrikam.com directly to Server2, you need to implement a solution that minimizes administrative effort.

What should you configure?

a. a secondary DNS zone

b. conditional forwarders

c. DNS Aliases (CNAME)

d. SRV records

22) You have an Azure subscription with two virtual networks: VNet1 in the US East region and VNet2 in the North Europe region. You have created a private DNS zone named Contoso.local and linked it to VNet1. To ensure that devices connected to VNet2 can resolve records in Contoso.local while minimizing administrative effort, you need to implement a solution.

What should you do?

A. Configure a peering between VNet1 and VNet2.

B. Create a virtual network gateway on each virtual network and configure Site-to-Site (S2S) VPN.

C. Create a DNS server on a virtual machine on each virtual network and configure conditional forwarding.

D. From Contoso.local, create a virtual network link to VNet2.

23) You have an Azure virtual network named VNet1 with an IP address space of 192.168.0.0/20. You deploy a virtual machine named VM1 to VNet1 and install the DNS Server role on VM1. You need to configure the DNS server on VM1 to forward DNS queries to Azure's recursive resolvers.

Which IP address should you use as the forwarder?

A. 168.63.129.16

B. 169.254.169.254

C. 192.168.0.2

D. 192.168.0.3

24) Your on-premises network includes an Active Directory Domain Services (AD DS) domain with a server named Server1 running Windows Server 2022. Additionally, you have a workgroup server named Server2 running Windows Server 2016 with the DNS Server role installed. After installing the IP Address Management (IPAM) feature on Server1, you need to manage DNS records on Server2 using IPAM from Server1 while minimizing administrative effort.

What should you do first?

A. From Server1, run a server discovery.

B. Join Server2 to the AD DS domain.

C. Modify the DNS server settings on Server2.

D. Upgrade Server2 to Windows Server 2022.

25) You have a server named Server1 running Windows Server with the DHCP Server role installed. You also have three Windows 11 devices: Computer1, Computer2, and Computer3. After running the Get-DhcpServerv4Reservation cmdlet, you receive the following output.

```
IPAddress       ScopeID        HostName                      AddressState

-----------     ------------   -----------                   --------------

10.0.25.15      10.0.25.0      computer1.contoso.com         ActiveReservation

10.0.25.17      10.0.25.0      computer2.contoso.com         ActiveReservation

10.0.25.18      10.0.25.0      computer3.contoso.com         Active
```

You decommission Computer1 and need to ensure that Computer3 is assigned the IP address 10.0.25.15.

Which two actions will achieve this goal?

Each correct answer provides a complete solution.

A. Delete the reservation for Computer1. Create a new reservation for the 10.0.25.15 IP address.

B. Delete the reservation for Computer1. From Computer3, run the ipconfig /renew command.

C. From the reservation for Computer1, change the IP address to 10.0.25.18.

D. From the reservation for Computer1, change the name to Computer3 and update the MAC address to match the MAC address of Computer3.

26) You have an Azure subscription with a virtual network named VNet1 and a subnet named Subnet1, which has an IP address range of 192.168.0.0/24. You plan to deploy a virtual machine named VM1 to Subnet1 and assign a static IP address to VM1. You need to determine the first available IP address that can be assigned to VM1 in Subnet1.

Which IP address should you identify?

A. 192.168.0.1

B. 192.168.0.2

C. 192.168.0.3

D. 192.168.0.4

27) Your on-premises network includes an Active Directory Domain Services (AD DS) domain along with several DHCP and DNS servers. You have deployed a new server named Server1

running Windows Server 2022 and installed the IP Address Management (IPAM) feature. You need to initiate a server discovery process on Server1.

What should you do first?

A. Deploy the IPAM settings to the DHCP and DNS servers by using a Group Policy Object (GPO).

B. Manually install the IPAM client on the existing DHCP and DNS servers.

C. On Server1, install the DHCP Server and DNS Server roles.

D. On Server1, open a PowerShell session and run the Invoke-IpamGpoProvisioning cmdlet.

28) You have an Azure subscription with a virtual network named VNet1. You need to set up connectivity to VNet1 using an ExpressRoute circuit, a Point-to-Site (P2S) VPN, and a Site-to-Site (S2S) VPN. The solution must ensure high availability for each type of connection.

What is the minimum number of virtual network gateways you should deploy to VNet1?

A. 1

B. 2

C. 3

D. 4

29) Your on-premises network includes a server named Server1 that hosts an application named App1, which utilizes Active Directory Federation Services (AD FS). Your perimeter

network has a server named Server2 running Windows Server. You need to securely make App1 accessible to internet users.

Which role should you install on Server2?

A. Network Controller

B. Web Server (IIS)

C. Network Policy and Access Services

D. Remote Access

30) You have an Azure subscription with a virtual network named VNet1 located in the East US region. You have also deployed an Azure Virtual WAN with a virtual hub named VHub1 in the East US region. You need to ensure that network traffic from VNet1 can connect to VHub1.

What should you create?

A. a Site-to-Site (S2S) VPN

B. a virtual network connection

C. a virtual network peering

D. an ExpressRoute Direct circuit

31) You have an Active Directory Domain Services (AD DS) domain with two domain controllers and 500 user accounts. An administrator executes a PowerShell script that removes the department names from all user accounts. You need to restore the department names while minimizing administrative effort. What action should you take?

A. Use the Active Directory Administrative Center to restore the user accounts via the Recycle Bin.

B. Restore a domain controller from a backup, then restart the domain controller.

C. Restore a domain controller from a backup, perform an Authoritative restore, and then restart the domain controller.

D. Restore a domain controller from a backup, perform a Nonauthoritative restore, and then restart the domain controller.

32) You manage an Active Directory Domain Services (AD DS) forest with two domains: amer.contoso.com and apac.contoso.com. In the apac.contoso.com domain, there is a domain local group called Group1, which includes users from the amer.contoso.com domain. When you check Group1's membership in Active Directory Users and Computers, the members are displayed as security identifiers (SIDs) instead of their usernames. The trust relationship between the two domains is confirmed to be fully functional. You need to ensure that the actual usernames are displayed instead of their SIDs.

Which FSMO role holder should you review?

A. domain naming

B. infrastructure

C. PDC emulator

D. RID

33) Your network includes an on-premises Active Directory

Domain Services (AD DS) domain called contoso.com. You also have an Azure subscription with a virtual machine named Server1 running Windows Server. You need to set up Server1 as a domain controller for contoso.com.

Which two actions should you perform? Each correct answer presents part of the solution.

A. Enable a managed identity for Server1.

B. Install the Active Directory Domain Services role on Server1 and promote Server1 to a domain controller.

C. Scale up Server1 to a larger virtual machine size to handle the AD DS load.

D. Set up a Site-to-Site (S2S) VPN between Server1 and the on-premises network.

34) The on-premises network includes an Active Directory Domain Services (AD DS) domain with two sites, named Site1 and Site2. Site1 has two domain controllers. You need to deploy a domain controller to Site2 while ensuring the solution meets the following criteria:

· Minimizes administrative effort.
· Maximizes security.

What should you deploy to Site2?

A. Microsoft Entra Domain Services

B. a domain controller in Azure

C. a read-only domain controller (RODC)

D. a replica domain controller

35) Your company has offices in New York and Seattle, connected via a dedicated WAN link. The network includes an Active Directory Domain Services (AD DS) domain with four domain controllers, two located in each office. You need to reduce the bandwidth used for replicating AD DS data between the offices. What should you do first?

A. Create an AD DS site for each office.

B. Enable the Bridge All Site Links (BASL) option.

C. Enable the global catalog role on each domain controller.

D. Run the repadmin /kcc command.

36) Your company's network includes an Active Directory Domain Services (AD DS) domain with four domain controllers. A new branch office is opening and will connect to the company network via a private WAN link. You plan to deploy two domain controllers at the new office. You need to minimize the Active Directory replication traffic over the WAN link. What should you do first?

A. Create a new site and subnet.

B. Create a site link.

C. Create a site link bridge.

D. Run the Knowledge Consistency Checker (KCC).

37) Your network includes an Active Directory Domain Services (AD DS) domain called contoso.com. A partner company, A. Datum Corp., has its own AD DS domain named adatum.com. You need to ensure that users from

adatum.com can access shared folders on specific file servers in contoso.com using their adatum.com user accounts. The solution must also ensure that users in contoso.com cannot access resources in adatum.com. What should you configure?

A. a one-way domain trust

B. a one-way forest trust with forest-wide authentication

C. a one-way forest trust with selective authentication

D. a two-way domain trust

E. a two-way forest trust

38) Your network includes two Active Directory Domain Services (AD DS) forests: contoso.com and fabrikam.com. The contoso.com forest has two domains: contoso.com and corp.contoso.com, while the fabrikam.com forest has a single domain. You need to create a group in the corp.contoso.com domain that includes users from all three domains. Which type of group should you create?

A. domain-local

B. global

C. universal

D. local

39) Your network has two Active Directory Domain Services (AD DS) forests: contoso.com and fabrikam.com. The contoso.com forest includes two domains: contoso.com and corp.contoso.com, while the fabrikam.com forest has a single domain. You need to create a group in the corp.contoso.com domain with the following requirements:

- It must include users from both contoso.com and corp.contoso.com.
- It must be used to grant permissions to resources in the fabrikam.com forest.

Which type of group should you use?

A. domain-local

B. local

C. global

D. universal

40) Your network includes an on-premises Active Directory Domain Services (AD DS) domain that syncs with a Microsoft Entra tenant. You need to ensure that when an on-premises user logs into Microsoft Entra, the authentication request is verified by an on-premises AD DS domain controller. The solution should require minimal administrative effort. What should you enable?

A. federation with Active Directory Federation Services (AD FS)

B. federation with PingFederate

C. pass-through authentication

D. password hash synchronization

41) Your network includes an on-premises Active Directory Domain Services (AD DS) domain named contoso.com, with the forest and domain functional levels set to Windows Server 2016 and all domain controllers running Windows Server 2022. You have a Microsoft Entra tenant. You need to synchronize contoso.com with the Microsoft Entra tenant

while ensuring that:

- All user management is handled within the AD DS domain.
- Authentication for cloud-based resources is performed through Microsoft Entra.

Which type of Microsoft Entra Connect configuration should you deploy?

A. Microsoft Entra Connect with password hash sync.

B. Microsoft Entra Connect with Active Directory Federation Services (AD FS).

C. Microsoft Entra Connect with password writeback.

D. Microsoft Entra Connect with group writeback.

E. Microsoft Entra Connect with pass-through authentication.

42) Your network includes an on-premises Active Directory Domain Services (AD DS) domain and a Microsoft Entra tenant. You need to set up synchronization between the AD DS domain and the Microsoft Entra tenant.

What should you do?

A. Deploy Microsoft Entra Connect to a server on the on-premises network.

B. Enable Microsoft Entra Domain Services for the Microsoft Entra tenant.

C. Install the Active Directory Domain Services role on an Azure virtual machine.

D. Set up a Site-to-Site (S2S) VPN between the on-premises network and the Azure network.

43) Your network includes an Active Directory Domain Services (AD DS) domain with an organizational unit (OU) named OU1 that syncs with a Microsoft Entra tenant. You need to stop accounts in OU1 from syncing with the Microsoft Entra tenant while minimizing administrative effort. What should you do?

A. From Microsoft Entra Connect, click Customize, and then clear the check box for OU1 on the Domain and OU filtering page.

B. From Microsoft Entra Connect, change the service account.

C. From Microsoft Entra Connect, click Refresh Directory Schema.

D. Run the Start-ADSyncSyncCycle -PolicyType Delta PowerShell command.

44) Your network includes an Active Directory Domain Services (AD DS) domain with 500 Windows 11 devices. You need to deploy applications and enforce security settings on these Windows 11 devices while minimizing administrative effort.

What should you use?

A. Group Policy Preferences

B. Local Policies

C. PowerShell

D. Windows packages

45) Your network includes an Active Directory Domain Services (AD DS) domain named contoso.com. You are planning to deploy new computers running Windows 11 Enterprise and need to update the Central Store for Group Policy Administrative Templates. Which two actions achieve the goal? Each correct answer presents a complete solution.

A. On a domain controller, copy the ADMX files to C:\Windows \System32\ PolicyDefinitions.

B. On a domain controller, copy the ADMX files to C:\Windows \SYSVOL\sysvol\contoso.com\Policies\PolicyDefinitions.

C. On a domain controller, copy the ADMX files to C:\Windows \PolicyDefinitions.

D. On a workstation, copy the ADMX files to \\contoso.com \SYSVOL\contoso.com\Policies\PolicyDefinitions.

E. On a workstation, copy the ADMX files to C:\Windows \PolicyDefinitions.

46) You have a Microsoft Entra Domain Services domain with 500 Windows 11 devices. You need to set up the password policies for the domain. What should you use?

A. Active Directory Users and Computers

B. Microsoft Entra Connect

C. Microsoft Entra Domain Services Configuration Wizard

D. Group Policy Management Console (GPMC)

47) You have a server named Server1 running Windows

Server 2022 Datacenter with the Hyper-V server role installed. Server1 hosts a virtual machine named VM1 that runs Windows Server 2019 Standard. You need to enable nested virtualization for VM1. What should you do first?

A. Enable dynamic memory for VM1.

B. Enable virtualization-based security (VBS) on Server1.

C. Shut down VM1.

D. Upgrade VM1 to Windows Server 2022.

48) You have a server named Server1 running Windows Server 2022 with the Hyper-V server role installed. Server1 hosts a virtual machine named VM1 that runs Windows Server 2022. After turning off VM1, you need to configure it to support nested virtualization. What should you do?

A. Start VM1.

B. From Server1, run the Set-VMProcessor cmdlet.

C. From Integration Services for VM1, enable Guest services.

D. From VM1, enable the Hyper-V server role.

49) You have an on-premises server named SVR1 running Windows Server with the Hyper-V server role installed. SVR1 hosts a virtual machine named VM1, which also has the Hyper-V server role installed. VM1's network interface is connected to an external switch on SVR1. You need to ensure that virtual machines connected to an external switch on VM1 can communicate with servers on the same network as SVR1. Which network virtualization feature should be enabled for SVR1?

A. Dynamic Virtual Machine Multi-Queue (d.VMMQ)

B. MAC address spoofing

C. Router guard

D. Single-root IO virtualization (SR-IOV)

50) You have an Azure virtual machine named VM1 with the Hyper-V server role installed. On VM1, you set up a nested virtual machine named VM2. You need to ensure that VM2 can communicate with virtual machines that are on the same virtual network as VM1. What should you do first?

A. Configure Router guard on the network adapter of VM2.

B. Create a NAT switch on VM1.

C. Create an external switch on VM1.

D. Enable MAC address spoofing on the network adapter of VM2.

ANSWERS AND EXPLANATIONS

1) To ensure that users in the Marketing OU can access storage1 and meet the technical requirements specified, you should consider how to handle identity synchronization and access management between on-premises Active Directory and Azure AD.

Answer: C. Azure AD Connect cloud sync

Explanation:

Azure AD Connect cloud sync (C): This is the appropriate solution for syncing user accounts and attributes from your on-premises Active Directory to Azure AD. It allows you to sync user data and ensure that Azure AD can recognize and manage the access for users in the Marketing OU. This solution is particularly useful for scenarios where you need to integrate with cloud resources while managing synchronization requirements.

Active Directory Federation Services (AD FS) (A): AD FS is used for federating identities and enabling single sign-on (SSO) between on-premises directories and cloud services. While it helps with authentication, it doesn't address the specific need to ensure that users in the Marketing OU have access to storage1.

Azure AD Connect in staging mode (B): This mode is used for testing synchronization configurations and is not intended for live use. It would not help in implementing the required access for users.

Azure AD Connect in active mode (D): This is the standard mode for synchronizing identities, but since the requirement involves specific Azure features and user management, Azure AD Connect cloud sync is more suited for this purpose, especially in a scenario involving cloud-based file shares.

Summary:

To ensure that users in the Marketing OU can access storage1 and meet the technical requirements, Azure AD Connect cloud sync (C) is the most appropriate choice.

2) For creating a new user in Active Directory Administrative Center, the correct required attributes are:

C. User SamAccountName logon

D. Full name

Explanation:

User SamAccountName logon (C): This is the logon name used to sign in to the domain and is a mandatory attribute when creating a user account.

Full name (D): This attribute is also required as it helps in identifying and managing the user account within Active Directory.

Other Attributes:

Password (A): While crucial for account creation, the password is not always required at the creation stage if the account can be set to require a password change on the next login.

Profile path (B): Optional and used for specifying a profile location.

First name (E): Useful but not mandatory for user creation.

User UPN logon (F): Not strictly required if the SamAccountName is provided, although UPN is often used for identifying users in the cloud.

In summary, User SamAccountName logon (C) and Full name (D) are the mandatory attributes when creating a new user in Active Directory Administrative Center.

3) Understanding the Requirements:

Enforce all Azure AD Password Protection policies: This means all password change attempts should be checked against the banned password list.

Automatic agent updates: The agent should be able to update itself without manual intervention.

Minimize administrative effort: The deployment and management should be as simple as possible.

Solution:

1. Install the Azure AD Password Protection agent on:

b. DC1 and DC2 only

Explanation:

The Azure AD Password Protection agent needs to be installed on all domain controllers to intercept password changes and check them against the banned password list.

RODC1 is not required as it doesn't hold the full copy of the directory.

2. Install the Azure AD Password Protection Proxy on:

d. Server1

Explanation:

The Azure AD Password Protection proxy is required to communicate with Azure AD and download the latest banned password list.

Since Server1 is the Azure AD Connect server, it's the most suitable choice for hosting the proxy. It likely already has network connectivity to the internet.

Note:

Ensure that Server1 has internet access to download updates and communicate with Azure AD.

Consider using a group managed service account (gMSA) for the Azure AD Password Protection proxy service to enhance security.

By following these steps, you'll ensure that all Azure AD Password Protection policies are enforced, agent updates are applied automatically, and administrative effort is minimized.

Reference:

https://learn.microsoft.com/en-us/entra/identity/authentication/howto-password-ban-bad-on-premises-deploy

4) The correct options are:

1. Attribute:

a. True

2. Tool:

b. Synchronization Rules Editor

Explanation:

Attribute:

True: When the cloudFiltered attribute is set to True, it indicates that the user should be excluded from synchronization. This configuration helps ensure that users with the NoSync custom attribute are not synchronized to Azure AD.

Tool:

Synchronization Rules Editor: This tool is used to configure synchronization rules to filter objects based on attributes. By using the Synchronization Rules Editor, you can set up rules to exclude users with specific attributes from being synchronized with Azure AD.

5) Correct answer: D. Turn on enhanced session mode.

Reasoning:

Enhanced session mode is a security feature in Windows that helps protect user credentials and data by isolating user sessions from the underlying operating system.

Given the context of the question focusing on VM2 and the requirement to fulfill "technical requirements," it's most likely that enhancing security and protecting user data is the primary goal.

While the other options are valid security measures, they

address different security concerns:

Shielded virtual machines: Protect virtual machines from administrator access.

Guest services integration service: Facilitates communication between the host and guest operating systems.

Credential Guard: Protects user credentials from unauthorized access.

Without more specific information about the technical requirements for VM2, turning on enhanced session mode is the most likely and generalizable solution.

6) Correct answer: A. 7

Based on the information provided, here's the breakdown of the password policies and their application:

Password Policies and Their Values:

Default Domain Policy: 10

Default Domain Controllers Policy: 12

Group Policy linked to OU1: 8

Password settings object applied to Group1: 14

Password settings object applied to User1: 7

Analysis:

In Active Directory, Group Policy Objects (GPOs) are applied in a specific order to determine the effective settings for a user or computer. The order of precedence is as follows:

Local Policies: Policies configured directly on the user or computer.

Group Policies: Policies linked to the user's organizational unit

(OU), groups, or the domain.

Default Domain Policy: The base policy for all domain objects.

In this case, User1 is a member of Group1 and resides in OU1. Therefore, the applicable GPOs are:

Default Domain Policy (10)

Group Policy linked to OU1 (8)

Password settings object applied to Group1 (14)

Password settings object applied to User1 (7)

Following the order of precedence, the Password settings object applied to User1 (7) takes priority.

Therefore, the minimum password length that User1 should use when changing to a new password is 7 characters.

Additional Considerations:

While the minimum password length is 7 characters, it's highly recommended to enforce stronger password policies, such as requiring a minimum password length of at least 12 characters, including uppercase and lowercase letters, numbers, and special characters.

Consider using password complexity requirements to further enhance password security.

7) To ensure that the Group Policy Object (GPO) named GPO1 applies only to the group named MemberServers, follow these steps:

1. Create the GPO:

Sign in to a domain-joined computer with administrative

privileges.

Open the Group Policy Management Console (GPMC).

Right-click the Group Policy Objects container and select New.

Name the new GPO GPO1 and click OK.

2. Edit the GPO:

Right-click GPO1 and select Edit to configure the desired settings.

3. Apply the GPO to the group:

In the Group Policy Management Console, locate GPO1.

Right-click on GPO1 and select Edit.

Go to the Scope tab.

In the Security Filtering section, remove the Authenticated Users group.

Click Add and enter MemberServers.

Click OK to add the group.

4. Ensure GPO Application:

Verify that the GPO settings are configured correctly and that the MemberServers group is the only one listed in the Security Filtering section.

Explanation:

GPO Creation and Configuration: Creating the GPO and configuring it involves administrative access and the use of the Group Policy Management Console to ensure the policy settings are correctly defined.

Security Filtering: By modifying the security filtering settings of the GPO, you control which groups or users the GPO will apply to. In this case, removing Authenticated Users and adding MemberServers ensures that only the computers in the MemberServers group receive the GPO settings.

8) To use the Azure Network Adapter for connecting on-premises servers to Azure resources, you need to meet certain prerequisites both on-premises and in Azure:

To configure the on-premises servers, use:

d. Windows Admin Center

Windows Admin Center is a powerful tool used for managing and configuring on-premises Windows servers. It provides a streamlined interface to configure network adapters and manage server settings that are essential for establishing connectivity with Azure.

To connect the Azure resources and Azure Network Adapter, use:

b. An Azure virtual network gateway

An Azure virtual network gateway is required to establish a secure and reliable connection between on-premises servers and Azure resources. It supports VPN connections and allows communication between your on-premises network and Azure Virtual Network.

Explanation:

Windows Admin Center: This tool simplifies the configuration and management of on-premises servers, including setting up network adapters required for Azure connectivity.

Azure virtual network gateway: This is essential for creating a secure connection from your on-premises environment to the Azure Virtual Network, enabling communication between your on-premises servers and Azure resources.

Other options like Azure CLI, Routing and Remote Access, Server Manager, Azure Bastion, Azure Firewall, private endpoints, and public Azure Load Balancers do not directly apply to the configuration of the Azure Network Adapter for this scenario.

9) Let's break down the steps to replace the expired certificate for Windows Admin Center:

Understanding the Process

To replace the expired certificate, we need to obtain a new one, configure it for IIS, and then update Windows Admin Center to use the new certificate.

Steps:

a. Obtain and install a new certificate.

Acquire a new certificate from your organization's Certificate Authority (CA).

Install the certificate on Server1.

f. Copy the certificate thumbprint.

Obtain the thumbprint of the newly installed certificate. This will be used to identify the certificate in the next step.

e. Run Windows Admin Center Setup and select Change.

Initiate the Windows Admin Center setup process and choose the "Change" option.

Provide the thumbprint of the new certificate during the setup.

Explanation:

We start by obtaining a new certificate and installing it on the server.

Next, we copy the thumbprint of the new certificate for reference.

Finally, we run the Windows Admin Center setup in change mode and provide the thumbprint of the new certificate to associate it with Windows Admin Center.

By following these steps, you'll successfully replace the expired certificate for Windows Admin Center.

10) To monitor Server1 using Azure Monitor, you need to set up the appropriate resources in your Azure subscription and install the necessary agent on Server1. Here's what you need to do:

Answer Area:

2. In the subscription, create:

b. A Log Analytics workspace

Explanation: Azure Monitor uses Log Analytics workspaces to collect and analyze data. You need to create a Log Analytics workspace to gather metrics and logs from Server1.

2. On Server1, install:

a. The Azure Monitor agent

Explanation: The Azure Monitor agent is required to send monitoring data from your on-premises server to the Log Analytics workspace in Azure.

Summary:

Create a Log Analytics workspace in your Azure subscription to store and analyze the monitoring data.

Install the Azure Monitor agent on Server1 to collect and send data to the Log Analytics workspace.

11) The first step you should take is:

B. Assign Admin1 the Azure Connected Machine Onboarding role for RG1.

Explanation:

Assigning Admin1 the Azure Connected Machine Onboarding role for the resource group RG1 is the first step because this role grants the necessary permissions to onboard and manage servers with Azure Arc. Without this role, Admin1 would not have the required permissions to perform the onboarding process, even if other steps like generating a script or hybrid joining the servers are done. Therefore, ensuring that Admin1 has the appropriate role is the foundational step to proceed with managing Server1 and Server2 using Azure Arc.

12) To set up resource-based constrained delegation, you need to use the Set-ADComputer cmdlet. The command should specify the computer account that will be allowed to delegate and the account to which it can delegate. Based on the scenario provided, you want to allow Server1 in contoso.com to delegate to Server2 in fabrikam.com.

The correct command is:

Set-ADComputer -Identity (Get-ADComputer server2.fabrikam.com) -PrincipalsAllowedToDelegateToAccount (Get-ADComputer server1.contoso.com)

Explanation:

Set-ADComputer -Identity: This specifies the account that will receive the delegation. Since Server2 hosts the resources that will be managed remotely, it should be the identity.

Correct option: b. (Get-ADComputer server2.fabrikam.com)

-PrincipalsAllowedToDelegateToAccount: This specifies the account that is allowed to delegate. Since Server1 will be performing the delegation using Windows Admin Center, it should be the principal allowed to delegate.

Correct option: a. (Get-ADComputer server1.contoso.com)

Putting it together, the full command is:

Set-ADComputer -Identity (Get-ADComputer server2.fabrikam.com) -PrincipalsAllowedToDelegateToAccount (Get-ADComputer server1.contoso.com)

13) To complete the PowerShell command for configuring Just Enough Administration (JEA) for helpdesk users to limit their usage of Hyper-V module cmdlets, you would use the Register-PSSessionConfiguration cmdlet and specify the session configuration file with the appropriate extension.

Here is how you should complete the command:

Register-PSSessionConfiguration -Path .\HyperVJeaConfig.pssc -Name 'HyperVJeaHelpDesk' -Force

Explanation:

Register-PSSessionConfiguration: This cmdlet is used to register a session configuration file, making it available for use.

Correct option: c. Register-PSSessionConfiguration

.pssc: This is the file extension for a PowerShell session configuration file, which is what you need to use with Register-PSSessionConfiguration.

Correct option: d. .pssc

Putting it together, the full command is:

Register-PSSessionConfiguration -Path .\HyperVJeaConfig.pssc -Name 'HyperVJeaHelpDesk' -Force

14) The correct answer is:

C. Configure VM1 to use a system-assigned managed identity.

Explanation:

To use the Azure Policy guest configuration feature for managing VM1, you need to enable a system-assigned managed identity. This identity allows Azure Policy to authenticate and apply policies to the virtual machine. Here's why the other options are not correct:

A. Add the PowerShell Desired State Configuration (DSC) extension to VM1: While DSC is used for configuration management, it is not specifically required for enabling Azure Policy guest configuration.

B. Configure VM1 to use a user-assigned managed identity: A user-assigned managed identity is not necessary for this scenario. A system-assigned managed identity is sufficient and simpler to configure.

D. Add the Custom Script Extension to VM1: This extension is used for running scripts on the VM but does not enable Azure Policy guest configuration.

By configuring VM1 to use a system-assigned managed identity, you provide the necessary permissions for Azure Policy to manage the VM.

15) To complete the command for creating an identity to

authenticate access to sub1 with the principle of least privilege, you should use the following:

(1) b. New-AzADServicePrincipal

(2) a. 'Azure Connected Machine Onboarding'

Explanation:

Identity Creation: You need a service principal to authenticate the script with Azure. The New-AzADServicePrincipal cmdlet creates a new service principal, which is appropriate for this purpose.

Role Assignment: The Azure Connected Machine Onboarding role is specifically designed for onboarding machines to Azure Arc. This role ensures the script has the required permissions for this task without giving excessive privileges.

Using these options adheres to the principle of least privilege by providing only the necessary permissions to perform the onboarding.

16) To manage VM1, which has only a private IP address, using Windows Admin Center from the Azure portal, you should configure:

B. a VPN connection to the virtual network that contains VM1.

Explanation:

Since VM1 has only a private IP address, it is not directly accessible from the internet. A VPN connection allows you to securely connect to the virtual network where VM1 is located from your Windows 11 computer. This enables you to manage VM1 using Windows Admin Center as if you were on the same network.

Here's why the other options are less suitable:

A. Azure Bastion: Azure Bastion is used to securely connect to VMs over the RDP/SSH protocol through the Azure portal. It does not specifically facilitate management of VMs via Windows Admin Center, which requires access to ports and services that Bastion doesn't handle.

C. Private Endpoint: A private endpoint provides a secure connection to Azure services, but it doesn't address direct VM management via Windows Admin Center. It's typically used for accessing PaaS resources securely.

D. NSG Rule: While an NSG rule allowing inbound traffic on port 443 might be necessary for allowing HTTPS traffic, it does not solve the issue of accessing VM1 from an external network if there's no direct route to the VM due to its private IP address.

17) To configure the branch office firewall to allow the necessary inbound connections to the Windows Admin Center gateway, you should allow:

A. 443

Explanation:

Windows Admin Center uses HTTPS for secure communication, which typically operates over TCP port 443. This port must be open on the firewall to allow the management traffic from the main office to reach the Windows Admin Center gateway installed in the branch office.

Here's why the other options are less suitable:

B. 3389: This port is used for Remote Desktop Protocol (RDP) and is not related to Windows Admin Center.

C. 5985: This port is used for Windows Remote Management (WinRM) over HTTP, which is not directly used by Windows Admin Center for its communication.

D. 6516: This port is used by some specific applications but is not used by Windows Admin Center.

18) To manage Microsoft updates on Server1 using Azure Arc, you should perform the following two actions:

A. From the Automation account, enable Update Management for Server1.

C. On Server1, install the Azure Monitor agent.

Explanation:

Enable Update Management (A): Update Management is a feature within the Azure Automation account that allows you to manage and deploy updates to servers. By enabling Update Management for Server1, you can start managing updates through Azure Arc.

Install the Azure Monitor agent (C): The Azure Monitor agent (formerly known as the Log Analytics agent) is required for collecting data and sending it to the Log Analytics workspace. This agent enables various monitoring and management features, including update management.

Here's why the other options are less relevant:

B. Connect Server1 from the Virtual machines data source of the Log Analytics workspace: This is not necessary for managing updates directly. Instead, the Azure Monitor agent handles data collection.

D. Add Microsoft Sentinel to the Log Analytics workspace:

Microsoft Sentinel is a security information and event management (SIEM) solution and is not directly related to managing Microsoft updates on servers.

19) To allow users to access WebApp1 using their Azure AD accounts while minimizing administrative effort, you should configure:

1. In Azure AD:

b. The Azure AD Application Proxy service

2. On-premises:

a. The Azure AD Application Proxy connector

Explanation:

Azure AD Application Proxy service (b): This service provides secure remote access to on-premises applications for users with Azure AD accounts. It allows for the integration of Azure AD authentication with your on-premises applications, including those using Kerberos authentication.

Azure AD Application Proxy connector (a): This connector needs to be installed on your on-premises environment to facilitate communication between Azure AD and your on-premises application, WebApp1. It ensures that authentication requests are properly routed to the application while enabling seamless Azure AD integration.

Using Azure AD Application Proxy minimizes administrative effort by leveraging existing Azure AD credentials and integrating them with your on-premises Kerberos-authenticated web applications.

20) To collect errors from the System event log of SRV1 and send

them to a Log Analytics workspace, you should perform the following steps:

1. Sign in to SRV1.

2. Install and configure the Azure Monitor agent (Log Analytics agent) on SRV1.

Explanation:

Sign in to SRV1: You need to access SRV1 to perform the necessary configurations. This involves either physically logging into SRV1 or using a remote management tool.

Install and configure the Azure Monitor agent: The Azure Monitor agent, formerly known as the Log Analytics agent, is required to collect and send log data to a Log Analytics workspace. You will need to install this agent on SRV1 and configure it to point to your Log Analytics workspace. This setup involves specifying the workspace ID and key and ensuring that the agent is configured to collect the System event log.

The source files located in \dc1.contoso.com\install might contain the necessary installer or configuration scripts for the Azure Monitor agent, so you will need to access this shared location from SRV1 to complete the setup.

21) To ensure that Server1 forwards all name resolution requests for fabrikam.com directly to Server2 while minimizing administrative effort, you should configure:

b. conditional forwarders

Explanation:

Conditional forwarders allow a DNS server to forward queries for specific DNS domains to designated DNS servers. In this case, you would configure Server1 to forward all DNS queries for the domain fabrikam.com to Server2. This setup ensures that any queries for fabrikam.com are directly sent to Server2, where the relevant DNS records are hosted, without affecting the resolution of other domains.

Here's why the other options are less suitable:

a. Secondary DNS zone: This option is used to create a read-only copy of a zone from another DNS server. It does not forward queries but rather replicates zone data.

c. DNS Aliases (CNAME): CNAME records are used to create aliases for domain names. They do not forward queries but rather map one domain name to another.

d. SRV records: SRV records are used to specify the location of services within a domain, such as LDAP or SIP. They do not handle forwarding DNS queries to other servers.

Extra explanation:

Incorrect - Secondary DNS zones provide an alternative DNS server for the zones they manage. The DNS data is read-only and updated from its master DNS server, which does not send all name resolution requests directly to the partner's DNS servers.

Correct - Conditional forwarders are a DNS feature that directs DNS queries based on the DNS domain name in the query. For example, you can configure a DNS server to forward all queries for names ending in widgets.example.com to a specific DNS server or multiple DNS servers.

Incorrect - DNS Aliases (CNAME) are used to assign multiple names (aliases) to a single system. This does not forward name resolution requests directly to the partner's DNS servers.

Incorrect - SRV records are used for service location, such as

LDAP for Active Directory Domain Services (AD DS). They do not handle forwarding name resolution requests to partner DNS servers.

22) To ensure that devices connected to VNet2 can resolve records in Contoso.local while minimizing administrative effort, you should:

D. From Contoso.local, create a virtual network link to VNet2.

Explanation:

Creating a virtual network link from the private DNS zone Contoso.local to VNet2 allows DNS resolution across both virtual networks. By linking the private DNS zone to both VNet1 and VNet2, you enable devices in VNet2 to resolve DNS records in the Contoso.local zone without additional configuration or complexity.

Here's why the other options are less suitable:

A. Configure peering between VNet1 and VNet2: Virtual network peering allows for connectivity between VNet1 and VNet2, but it does not automatically propagate DNS zones or settings between them.

B. Create a virtual network gateway on each virtual network and configure Site-to-Site (S2S) VPN: This approach is more complex and typically used for connecting on-premises networks or different Azure regions rather than for internal DNS resolution across virtual networks.

C. Create a DNS server on a virtual machine on each virtual network and configure conditional forwarding: This option adds administrative overhead and complexity. Using virtual network links is a more straightforward and integrated solution for DNS resolution in Azure.

Reference:

https://learn.microsoft.com/en-us/windows-server/
networking/technologies/ipam/add-a-dns-resource-record

23) To configure the DNS server on VM1 to forward DNS queries
to Azure's recursive resolvers, you should use:

A. 168.63.129.16

Explanation:

168.63.129.16 is the IP address of Azure's internal DNS resolver,
which can be used for forwarding DNS queries to Azure's
recursive DNS servers. This IP address is a well-known address
used by Azure services to handle DNS queries and is specifically
intended for DNS resolution within Azure virtual networks.

Here's why the other options are not suitable:

B. 169.254.169.254: This address is used for the Azure Instance
Metadata Service (IMDS), which provides information about the
virtual machine and is not related to DNS resolution.

C. 192.168.0.2 and D. 192.168.0.3: These addresses are within
the IP address space of your virtual network (192.168.0.0/20)
and would typically be used for internal resources within your
VNet, not for forwarding to external or Azure recursive DNS
resolvers.

24) For IPAM to manage DNS records on Server2 from Server1, B.
Join Server2 to the AD DS domain is indeed the correct approach.

Explanation:

IPAM in Windows Server is designed to manage DNS servers that are part of an AD DS domain. Server2 needs to be joined to the AD DS domain to integrate with the IPAM infrastructure and enable centralized management of DNS records.

Here's why the other options are less suitable:

A. Run a server discovery from Server1: Server discovery is part of the process but only works for servers that are already domain-joined or properly configured for management.

C. Modify DNS server settings on Server2: While necessary for configuration, Server2 must first be part of the AD DS domain to allow IPAM management.

D. Upgrade Server2 to Windows Server 2022: Upgrading is not required if the goal is to manage DNS records from an AD DS domain, as joining the domain is sufficient.

25) Correct answer: AD

A. Correct – This action replaces the DHCP reservation for Computer1 with a new reservation for Computer3, ensuring Computer3 receives the IP address 10.0.25.15.

B. Incorrect – Simply deleting the reservation for Computer1 and then running ipconfig /renew on Computer3 does not guarantee that Computer3 will be assigned the IP address 10.0.25.15.

C. Incorrect – Modifying the reservation for Computer1 to use the IP address 10.0.25.18 does not fulfill the requirement of assigning the IP address 10.0.25.15 to Computer3.

D. Correct – Updating the reservation details from Computer1 to Computer3 with the new IP address assignment of 10.0.25.15

will meet the requirement.

26) Correct answer: D. 192.168.0.4 is the correct answer.

Here's why:

In a subnet with the IP range 192.168.0.0/24:

192.168.0.0 is reserved as the network address.

192.168.0.1 is often reserved for the default gateway or other network infrastructure.

192.168.0.2 and 192.168.0.3 might be reserved for other services or devices.

Therefore, 192.168.0.4 is the first IP address available for assignment to VM1 in this subnet.

Azure reserves the first four IP addresses in each subnet address range, so these addresses cannot be assigned to resources. Consequently, the first IP address that can be assigned to a network interface of an Azure virtual machine in a subnet with an IP address range of 192.168.0.0/24 is 192.168.0.4.

27) Correct answer: D. On Server1, open a PowerShell session and run the Invoke-IpamGpoProvisioning cmdlet is indeed the correct first step for initiating a server discovery process with IPAM.

Explanation:

Invoke-IpamGpoProvisioning Cmdlet: This cmdlet is used to create and apply the necessary Group Policy Objects (GPOs) that configure the DHCP and DNS servers for IPAM management.

By running this cmdlet, you set up the IPAM settings on your network infrastructure, enabling Server1 to discover and manage the DHCP and DNS servers.

Here's why the other options are less suitable:

A. Deploy the IPAM settings to the DHCP and DNS servers by using a Group Policy Object (GPO): While this is ultimately necessary, the Invoke-IpamGpoProvisioning cmdlet automates and streamlines this process, making it the first step to enable server discovery.

B. Manually install the IPAM client on the existing DHCP and DNS servers: This is not required since IPAM uses GPOs to manage settings rather than a client installation.

C. Install the DHCP Server and DNS Server roles on Server1: Not relevant for the discovery process; Server1 does not need to host these roles to manage other servers.

Running the Invoke-IpamGpoProvisioning cmdlet is the proper initial step to set up IPAM management on your network.

28) Correct answer B. 2

Explanation:

To ensure high availability for each type of connection—ExpressRoute, Point-to-Site (P2S) VPN, and Site-to-Site (S2S) VPN—you need to deploy at least two virtual network gateways in VNet1.

Here's why:

ExpressRoute Circuit: Requires a dedicated virtual network gateway to handle the ExpressRoute connection.

Point-to-Site (P2S) VPN: Also requires a virtual network gateway to handle the P2S VPN connections.

Site-to-Site (S2S) VPN: Requires a separate virtual network gateway for handling S2S VPN connections.

In Azure, high availability for these connections typically involves deploying a VPN gateway (for P2S and S2S VPN) and an ExpressRoute gateway. Although it's possible to use a single VPN gateway for both P2S and S2S VPN connections, separating them into two distinct gateways ensures better high availability and redundancy.

Summary:

1 Gateway (not sufficient): A single gateway can handle either ExpressRoute or VPN connections, but not both, especially with high availability.

2 Gateways: One gateway for ExpressRoute and one for VPN (both P2S and S2S), providing high availability for all connections.

3 Gateways: More than necessary; although it could be used if separating P2S and S2S VPN connections into different gateways for even more redundancy, it's not the minimum requirement.

4 Gateways: More than necessary and adds complexity without additional benefit over 2 gateways.

Thus, deploying at least 2 gateways (one for ExpressRoute and one for VPN) meets the requirement for high availability for each connection type.

29) D. Remote Access

Explanation:

To securely publish an application that uses Active Directory Federation Services (AD FS) to internet users, you should use a role that allows you to set up secure access and manage external connections. The Remote Access role includes the Web Application Proxy feature, which is specifically designed to securely publish internal applications, including those using AD FS, to external users.

Here's why the other options are less suitable:

A. Network Controller: This role is used for managing network infrastructure, but it is not designed for securely publishing applications.

B. Web Server (IIS): While IIS can host web applications, it does not provide the specific features needed to securely publish internal applications to the internet or manage AD FS connections.

C. Network Policy and Access Services: This role is used for managing network policies and access services, such as VPNs, but it does not provide the functionality needed to securely publish web applications.

Remote Access with Web Application Proxy is the appropriate role to install on Server2 for securely publishing App1 and ensuring secure access for internet users.

30) B. a virtual network connection

Explanation:

To enable network traffic from a virtual network (VNet1) to reach a Virtual WAN hub (VHub1), you need to create a virtual network connection. This connection links the virtual network to the Azure Virtual WAN, allowing network traffic to flow between the two.

Here's why the other options are less suitable:

A. a Site-to-Site (S2S) VPN: This is used to connect an on-premises network to an Azure virtual network, not for connecting a virtual network directly to a Virtual WAN hub.

C. a virtual network peering: This allows direct connectivity between two Azure VNets but does not involve Azure Virtual WAN. Peering is not used for connecting a VNet to a Virtual WAN hub.

D. an ExpressRoute Direct circuit: This provides a private, high-bandwidth connection between an on-premises network and Azure. It is not necessary for connecting a VNet to a Virtual WAN hub if you are only working within Azure resources.

Creating a virtual network connection to link VNet1 with VHub1 is the correct approach to ensure network traffic from VNet1 can reach the Virtual WAN hub.

31) Answer: C. Restore a domain controller from a backup, perform an Authoritative restore, and then restart the domain controller.

Explanation:

An Authoritative restore is the best solution for this scenario because it allows you to restore specific objects or attributes, such as the department names, to their previous state. By performing an Authoritative restore on a domain controller, you can ensure that the restored data, in this case, the department names, is replicated to all other domain controllers in the domain. This approach minimizes administrative effort since it precisely targets the required data without affecting the entire domain or user accounts.

32) Answer: B. Infrastructure

Explanation:

The Infrastructure Master FSMO (Flexible Single Master Operations) role is responsible for updating references from objects in its domain to objects in other domains. When a user from a different domain is added to a group, the Infrastructure Master ensures that the correct information (such as usernames) is displayed instead of security identifiers (SIDs). If members of Group1 are showing as SIDs, it suggests that the Infrastructure Master is not properly updating the cross-domain references. Reviewing the Infrastructure Master role holder for any issues would be the correct step to ensure that usernames are displayed instead of SIDs.

33) Answer: B. Install the Active Directory Domain Services role on Server1 and promote Server1 to a domain controller.

D. Set up a Site-to-Site (S2S) VPN between Server1 and the on-premises network.

Explanation:

To configure Server1 as a domain controller for the on-premises AD DS domain (contoso.com), you need to:

B. Install the Active Directory Domain Services role on Server1 and promote Server1 to a domain controller: This step is necessary to turn Server1 into a domain controller within the existing contoso.com domain.

D. Set up a Site-to-Site (S2S) VPN between Server1 and the on-premises network: A Site-to-Site VPN is required to securely connect the Azure virtual network, where Server1 resides, with the on-premises network. This connection allows Server1 to communicate with the existing domain controllers in contoso.com, enabling it to join the domain and replicate AD DS information.

Options A and C are not required for promoting Server1 to a domain controller in this scenario.

34) Answer: C. A read-only domain controller (RODC)

Explanation:

Deploying a read-only domain controller (RODC) to Site2 is the best choice to meet the requirements of minimizing administrative effort and maximizing security.

Security: An RODC contains a read-only copy of the Active Directory database, which reduces the risk of unauthorized changes being made to the directory. This is particularly useful in remote or less secure locations, like Site2, where physical security might be a concern.

Administrative Effort: An RODC requires less administrative management compared to a writable domain controller since it doesn't handle updates or changes directly and instead forwards them to a writable domain controller in Site1.

This setup provides the necessary AD DS services at Site2 while keeping security high and administrative overhead low.

35) Answer: A. Create an AD DS site for each office.

Explanation:

To reduce the bandwidth used for replicating AD DS data

between the offices, you should first create an Active Directory site for each office.

Creating AD DS Sites: By defining sites in Active Directory, you can control and optimize replication traffic. Sites allow you to configure replication schedules, define site links, and control the frequency and timing of replication. This setup ensures that replication traffic is minimized by allowing domain controllers within the same site to replicate more frequently, and reduces the replication load over the WAN link between the offices.

Options B, C, and D are not directly related to minimizing replication bandwidth between sites:

B. Enable the Bridge All Site Links (BASL) option: This option is typically used to enable replication across all site links, which is not specifically aimed at minimizing bandwidth.

C. Enable the global catalog role on each domain controller: While enabling the global catalog role can improve search performance and availability, it does not directly address bandwidth optimization for replication.

D. Run the repadmin /kcc command: This command forces the Knowledge Consistency Checker (KCC) to recalculate the replication topology, but it does not directly impact the optimization of replication bandwidth.

36) Answer: A. Create a new site and subnet.

Explanation:

To minimize Active Directory replication traffic over the WAN link, the first step is to create a new site and subnet for the new branch office.

Creating a New Site and Subnet: By creating a new site and

subnet for the branch office, you can define the replication topology specifically for that location. This allows you to configure replication schedules and site link costs tailored to the new office, ensuring that replication traffic is minimized and occurs according to the defined policies.

Options B, C, and D are not the first steps for minimizing replication traffic:

B. Create a site link: While creating site links is part of the process, it is not the first step. The site and subnet must be created first to properly associate with the site link.

C. Create a site link bridge: Site link bridges are used to connect multiple site links to allow for replication across those links. This is more relevant after initial site and site link configuration.

D. Run the Knowledge Consistency Checker (KCC): The KCC is used to generate and maintain the replication topology but does not directly impact the minimization of replication traffic until the site and site link configurations are in place.

37) Answer: C. A one-way forest trust with selective authentication

Explanation:

To achieve the requirements:

Users from adatum.com can access shared folders on specific file servers in contoso.com.

Users in contoso.com cannot access resources in adatum.com.

You should configure a one-way forest trust with selective authentication.

Here's why:

One-way Forest Trust: This type of trust allows users in

the trusting domain (contoso.com) to access resources in the trusted domain (adatum.com), but not the other way around. This aligns with your requirement that users from adatum.com should access resources in contoso.com, but not the other way around.

Selective Authentication: This setting allows you to specify which users or groups in the trusted domain (adatum.com) can access resources in the trusting domain (contoso.com). It provides granular control over access and ensures that only specified users from adatum.com can access the shared folders, meeting the requirement of restricting access for contoso.com users to adatum.com resources.

Options Analysis:

A. A one-way domain trust: This could allow access from adatum.com to contoso.com, but it does not provide the granularity needed for selective access control.

B. A one-way forest trust with forest-wide authentication: This would allow all users in adatum.com to access all resources in contoso.com, which does not meet your requirement of restricting access to specific file servers.

D. A two-way domain trust: This would allow users from both domains to access resources in each domain, which is contrary to your requirement of restricting access.

E. A two-way forest trust: Similar to a two-way domain trust, this allows users from both domains to access resources in both directions, which does not meet the requirement of limiting access.

38) Correct answer: A. Domain-local

A. Correct – Domain-local group members can be from any

domain within their local AD DS forest or any trusted forests.

B. Incorrect – Global groups can only include users from the same domain.

C. Incorrect – Local groups are not created within a domain; they are created in the local SAM database on individual servers.

D. Incorrect – Universal groups can include users from any domain within the same forest or trusted forests, not just from the same forest.

39) The correct answer for this scenario is:

D. Universal

Here's why:

Domain-local groups (A): These groups can only contain members from the same domain (corp.contoso.com in this case). They wouldn't work because you need users from both contoso.com and corp.contoso.com.

Local groups (B): These are similar to domain-local groups but have an even more limited scope, typically to a specific computer. They're not suitable for domain-wide access.

Global groups (C): These groups can include members from within the same forest (contoso.com) and any trusted domains (like fabrikam.com). However, they cannot include members from untrusted forests. If the contoso.com forest is not explicitly trusted with fabrikam.com, global groups wouldn't work.

Universal groups (D) are the ideal choice because they can encompass members from:

Any domain within a trusted forest (contoso.com in this situation).

Any trusted domain (fabrikam.com).

This flexibility allows you to include users from both contoso.com and corp.contoso.com while granting them permissions to resources in the fabrikam.com forest.

Additional considerations:

Trust relationships: Ensure a two-way trust exists between contoso.com and fabrikam.com for seamless user access across domains.

Group scope: Universal groups are typically stored in the root domain of the forest. However, you can create them in any writable domain as long as the domain controller has a universal group object class.

Permissions: Carefully assign permissions to the universal group based on the resources in fabrikam.com it needs to access and the security principles you want to enforce.

By choosing a universal group and establishing trust relationships, you can effectively manage access to resources across different forests in your network.

40) Answer: C. Pass-through authentication

Explanation:

To ensure that when an on-premises user logs into Microsoft Entra, the authentication request is validated by an on-premises AD DS domain controller, and to minimize administrative effort, you should enable pass-through authentication.

Pass-through Authentication: This method allows users to authenticate directly against your on-premises Active Directory when they log in to Microsoft Entra. It ensures that the authentication request is validated by an on-premises domain controller, without requiring any complex federation setup. This method is simpler to configure and manage compared to other options.

Options Analysis:

A. Federation with Active Directory Federation Services (AD FS): AD FS is a more complex solution that provides single sign-on (SSO) and federation capabilities. It involves setting up additional infrastructure and configurations, which can be more administratively intensive.

B. Federation with PingFederate: Similar to AD FS, PingFederate is a third-party federation solution that provides SSO and federation but requires more setup and management.

D. Password hash synchronization: This method synchronizes password hashes from on-premises AD to Microsoft Entra. While it allows users to authenticate using Microsoft Entra, it does not ensure that authentication requests are validated by an on-premises domain controller.

Therefore, pass-through authentication is the best choice for ensuring authentication requests are verified by an on-premises domain controller with minimal administrative effort.

41) Correct answer: A. Microsoft Entra Connect with password hash sync.

Microsoft Entra Connect with password hash synchronization meets the requirement because it synchronizes users to the Microsoft Entra tenant along with their password hashes, ensuring that user objects are managed in the local AD DS domain. When synchronized users access cloud resources, Microsoft Entra can authenticate them using the stored password hashes.

In contrast, AD FS ensures users are always authenticated by the local AD DS, but requires a more complex setup. Features like password writeback, group writeback, and pass-through authentication involve managing user attributes from Microsoft Entra, which is not necessary for your scenario.

42) Answer: A. Deploy Microsoft Entra Connect to a server on the on-premises network

Explanation:

To set up synchronization between an on-premises Active Directory Domain Services (AD DS) domain and a Microsoft Entra tenant, you should deploy Microsoft Entra Connect to a server on your on-premises network.

Here's why:

Microsoft Entra Connect is the tool specifically designed to synchronize user accounts, groups, and other directory data between an on-premises AD DS and Microsoft Entra (Azure AD). It ensures that users and attributes from the on-premises AD DS domain are synchronized to the Microsoft Entra tenant.

Options Analysis:

B. Enable Microsoft Entra Domain Services for the Microsoft Entra tenant: This option is used to provide managed domain services such as domain join, group policy, and LDAP/NTLM authentication in the cloud. It does not synchronize on-premises AD data to Microsoft Entra.

C. Install the Active Directory Domain Services role on an Azure virtual machine: Installing AD DS on an Azure VM would set up a new domain controller in Azure, which is not necessary for synchronizing your existing on-premises AD DS with Microsoft

Entra.

D. Set up a Site-to-Site (S2S) VPN between the on-premises network and the Azure network: While a VPN connection might be required for certain scenarios involving network communication between on-premises and Azure resources, it is not used for synchronizing directory data.

Therefore, deploying Microsoft Entra Connect is the correct and most efficient method for synchronizing your on-premises AD DS domain with the Microsoft Entra tenant.

43) Answer: A. From Microsoft Entra Connect, click Customize, and then clear the check box for OU1 on the Domain and OU filtering page.

Explanation:

To prevent accounts in the organizational unit (OU) named OU1 from syncing with the Microsoft Entra tenant, you should modify the synchronization settings in Microsoft Entra Connect.

Here's how:

Option A: This involves accessing Microsoft Entra Connect, selecting "Customize," and then clearing the check box for OU1 on the Domain and OU filtering page. This action will exclude OU1 from the synchronization process, ensuring that accounts within that OU do not sync with Microsoft Entra.

Options Analysis:

B. From Microsoft Entra Connect, change the service account: Changing the service account will not affect which OUs are synced. The service account is used for authentication and does not control synchronization settings.

EXAM AZ-800: ADMINISTERING WINDOWS SERVER HYBRID CORE INFRAST...

C. From Microsoft Entra Connect, click Refresh Directory Schema: Refreshing the directory schema updates the schema information but does not change synchronization settings or filtering.

D. Run the Start-ADSyncSyncCycle -PolicyType Delta PowerShell command: This command initiates a delta sync cycle to apply recent changes but does not modify synchronization filters or exclude specific OUs from syncing.

Therefore, to stop accounts in OU1 from syncing with Microsoft Entra and to minimize administrative effort, option A is the correct choice.

44) Answer: A. Group Policy Preferences

Explanation:

To deploy applications and enforce security settings on 500 Windows 11 devices while minimizing administrative effort, Group Policy Preferences is the most appropriate tool.

Here's why:

Group Policy Preferences allows you to configure settings and deploy applications to multiple computers in a domain efficiently. You can use it to manage a wide range of settings, including software deployment, security configurations, and more, across all Windows 11 devices in the domain. This approach centralizes management and simplifies the process, making it suitable for handling large numbers of devices.

Options Analysis:

B. Local Policies: Local policies are configured on individual devices and do not scale well for managing multiple devices in a domain. They require manual configuration on each device, which is not ideal for managing 500 devices.

C. PowerShell: While PowerShell can be used to deploy applications and enforce settings, it requires scripting and manual execution. It is less efficient for large-scale deployment and management compared to Group Policy.

D. Windows packages: Windows packages (such as MSIs or app installers) are used to install applications but do not provide a comprehensive solution for enforcing security settings. They also require additional tools or manual intervention for large-scale deployments.

Thus, Group Policy Preferences is the best choice for efficiently deploying applications and enforcing security settings across a large number of Windows 11 devices in an Active Directory domain.

45) Answer: B. On a domain controller, copy the ADMX files to C: \Windows\SYSVOL\sysvol\contoso.com\Policies \PolicyDefinitions.

D. On a workstation, copy the ADMX files to \contoso.com \SYSVOL\contoso.com\Policies\PolicyDefinitions.

Explanation:

To update the Central Store for Group Policy Administrative Templates in an Active Directory environment, you need to ensure that the ADMX files are placed in the correct location. Here's how to achieve this:

Option B: On a domain controller, copy the ADMX files to C: \Windows\SYSVOL\sysvol\contoso.com\Policies \PolicyDefinitions. This is the location of the Central Store for Group Policy Administrative Templates. By copying the ADMX files here, they become available for all domain controllers and

Group Policy Management tools.

Option D: On a workstation, copy the ADMX files to \ \contoso.com\SYSVOL\contoso.com\Policies\PolicyDefinitions. This is another way to update the Central Store, where the ADMX files are stored on the network share that is accessible to all domain controllers and workstations. This path is shared across the network and used by Group Policy Management tools to access the Central Store.

Options Analysis:

A. On a domain controller, copy the ADMX files to C:\Windows \System32\PolicyDefinitions: This location is for local policy definitions on the individual machine and is not used for the Central Store in a domain environment.

C. On a domain controller, copy the ADMX files to C:\Windows \PolicyDefinitions: This is also a local path and not the Central Store location for ADMX files.

E. On a workstation, copy the ADMX files to C:\Windows \PolicyDefinitions: This updates the local policy definitions on that workstation, not the Central Store used by the domain.

Therefore, the correct answers for updating the Central Store for Group Policy Administrative Templates are B and D.

46) Answer: D. Group Policy Management Console (GPMC)

Explanation:

To configure password policies for a Microsoft Entra Domain Services domain, you should use the Group Policy Management Console (GPMC). Here's why:

Group Policy Management Console (GPMC): This tool allows you to create and manage Group Policy Objects (GPOs) that control various settings, including password policies, for the domain. In Microsoft Entra Domain Services, password policies are configured through GPOs applied to the domain.

Options Analysis:

A. Active Directory Users and Computers: This tool is primarily used for managing user accounts and other directory objects. It does not handle the configuration of domain-wide password policies.

B. Microsoft Entra Connect: This tool is used for synchronizing on-premises Active Directory with Microsoft Entra (Azure AD). It does not configure domain password policies.

C. Microsoft Entra Domain Services Configuration Wizard: This wizard is used to set up and configure Microsoft Entra Domain Services, but not for configuring domain password policies.

Therefore, to set up password policies for a Microsoft Entra Domain Services domain, you should use the Group Policy Management Console (GPMC).

47) Answer: C. Shut down VM1.

Explanation:

To enable nested virtualization on a virtual machine (VM1) running Windows Server 2019 Standard, you need to perform the following steps:

Shut down VM1: Nested virtualization requires that the VM be powered off before you can modify its settings. This is necessary because the virtual CPU settings need to be adjusted while the VM is not running.

Options Analysis:

A. Enable dynamic memory for VM1: This action is unrelated to nested virtualization. Dynamic memory settings manage the allocation of memory to the VM but do not affect virtualization features.

B. Enable virtualization-based security (VBS) on Server1: VBS is used for securing the host operating system and does not impact nested virtualization settings. Nested virtualization involves configuring the VM to use the virtualization extensions of the host CPU.

D. Upgrade VM1 to Windows Server 2022: While Windows Server 2022 might have enhanced support for virtualization, you can enable nested virtualization on Windows Server 2019 as well. An upgrade is not necessary for this feature.

Therefore, shutting down VM1 is the first step required to enable nested virtualization. After shutting down the VM, you can modify its settings to enable nested virtualization and then restart it.

48) Answer: B. From Server1, run the Set-VMProcessor cmdlet.

Explanation:

To configure VM1 to support nested virtualization, you need to enable the virtualization extensions on the VM. This is done using the Set-VMProcessor cmdlet from the Hyper-V host (Server1).

Here's how it works:

B. From Server1, run the Set-VMProcessor cmdlet: This cmdlet allows you to modify the processor settings for VM1. To enable nested virtualization, you use the -

ExposeVirtualizationExtensions parameter to expose the virtualization extensions to VM1, which is necessary for nested virtualization.

Options Analysis:

A. Start VM1: Starting VM1 is not required to enable nested virtualization. In fact, VM1 needs to be turned off while you configure its settings.

C. From Integration Services for VM1, enable Guest services: This option is related to enabling services that interact with the guest operating system, not configuring nested virtualization.

D. From VM1, enable the Hyper-V server role: This is not necessary for enabling nested virtualization. Enabling nested virtualization involves configuring settings on the host (Server1), not installing Hyper-V inside VM1.

Therefore, the correct action to configure VM1 to support nested virtualization is to run the Set-VMProcessor cmdlet from Server1.

49) Answer: B. MAC address spoofing

Explanation:

To ensure that virtual machines connected to an external switch on VM1 can communicate with servers on the same network as SVR1, you need to enable MAC address spoofing. This feature allows the virtual machines to use arbitrary MAC addresses, which is necessary when the virtual machines need to appear as though they are on the same network as SVR1 and communicate with external networks.

Options Analysis:

A. Dynamic Virtual Machine Multi-Queue (d.VMMQ): This feature improves network performance by allowing a single network adapter to handle multiple queues. It does not address the issue of network communication between virtual machines and servers on the same network.

C. Router guard: This feature is used to protect against rogue DHCP servers and does not affect the ability of virtual machines to communicate with the external network.

D. Single-root IO virtualization (SR-IOV): This technology enhances network and storage performance by allowing multiple virtual machines to share a physical network adapter more efficiently. However, it does not impact the ability of virtual machines to communicate with external networks.

Therefore, enabling MAC address spoofing on SVR1 is necessary to ensure that virtual machines connected to an external switch on VM1 can communicate with servers on the same network as SVR1.

50) Answer: B. Create a NAT switch on VM1

Explanation:

To ensure that the nested virtual machine VM2 can communicate with virtual machines on the same virtual network as VM1, you should create a NAT switch on VM1. Here's why:

B. Create a NAT switch on VM1: By creating a NAT (Network Address Translation) switch on VM1, you can configure VM1 to act as a router, allowing VM2 to use NAT to communicate with other virtual machines on the same virtual network as VM1. This setup enables VM2 to access the network and resources outside its own virtual network.

Options Analysis:

A. Configure Router guard on the network adapter of VM2: Router guard is used to protect against rogue DHCP servers and does not facilitate communication between nested virtual machines and other VMs on the same network.

C. Create an external switch on VM1: An external switch connects virtual machines to the physical network but may not provide the necessary NAT configuration for communication between nested VMs and other VMs on the same virtual network.

D. Enable MAC address spoofing on the network adapter of VM2: While MAC address spoofing is important for allowing VMs to use arbitrary MAC addresses, it does not address the need for NAT configuration to facilitate communication between VM2 and VMs on the same virtual network.

Therefore, creating a NAT switch on VM1 is the first step to ensure that VM2 can communicate with virtual machines on the same virtual network as VM1.

Feel free to reach out to me anytime, and don't forget to connect with me on LinkedIn: Georgio Daccache. I'm always available to provide additional assistance and support.

Good Luck

www.ingramcontent.com/pod-product-compliance
Lightning Source LLC
Chambersburg PA
CBHW071248050326
40690CB00011B/2310